LEEDS UNITED
IN THE 21ST CENTURY

LEEDS UNITED
IN THE 21ST CENTURY

DAVE TOMLINSON

AMBERLEY

Cover images:

16 April 2016 – The fans make their views clear before the match against Reading. (Copyright Heidi Haigh)

On Wesley Street, the other side of Elland Road. (Copyright Andy McVeigh, The Burley Banksy www.burleybanksy.com)

August 2020 – Champions 2020 mural at Elland Road by Mateusz Klich. (Copyright Dave Tomlinson)

First published 2021

Amberley Publishing
The Hill, Stroud
Gloucestershire, GL5 4EP

www.amberley-books.com

Copyright © Dave Tomlinson 2021

The right of Dave Tomlinson to be identified as the Author of this work has been asserted in accordance with the Copyright, Designs and Patents Act 1988.

All rights reserved. No part of this book may be reprinted or reproduced or utilised in any form or by any electronic, mechanical or other means, now known or hereafter invented, including photocopying and recording, or in any information storage or retrieval system, without the permission in writing from the Publishers.

British Library Cataloguing in Publication Data.
A catalogue record for this book is available from the British Library.

ISBN 978 1 3981 0840 0 (paperback)
ISBN 978 1 3981 0841 7 (ebook)

1 2 3 4 5 6 7 8 9 10

Typeset in 10pt on 12pt Sabon.
Typesetting by SJmagic DESIGN SERVICES, India.
Printed in Great Britain.

Contents

Prologue	7
Chapter One: Living the Dream	8
Chapter Two: The Cracks Begin to Show	12
Chapter Three: The Mighty Fall	17
Chapter Four: Cheer Up Peter Reid	24
Chapter Five: Club for Sale	32
Chapter Six: Just Me and Gary Kelly	38
Chapter Seven: Ken Bates	45
Chapter Eight: Dead Cat Bounce	50
Chapter Nine: The Stuff of Nightmares	58
Chapter Ten: Into the Abyss	64
Chapter Eleven: Fifteen Points, We Don't Give a F***!	72
Chapter Twelve: Return of the Mac	77
Chapter Thirteen: Simon Grayson	84
Chapter Fourteen: Missing the Boat	94
Chapter Fifteen: Warnock	103
Chapter Sixteen: GFH Capital	107

Chapter Seventeen: Cellino	111
Chapter Eighteen: The Italian Job	116
Chapter Nineteen: Becalmed	122
Chapter Twenty: New Kids on the Block	126
Chapter Twenty-One: The Genius on the Blue Bucket	130
Chapter Twenty-Two: We Go Again	141
Chapter Twenty-Three: The Stubborn Idealist	149
Chapter Twenty-Four: Bye Bye Big Six	153
Bibliography	159

Prologue

7.30 p.m., Friday 17 July 2020.

Huddersfield Town's winning goal in the final few minutes of their game against West Bromwich Albion secures the victory that almost certainly ensures their survival in the Championship.

For the really big news of the evening, however, you had to travel 16 miles down the M621 to Elland Road, Leeds, where there was a party to end all parties.

The points dropped by Albion meant that Leeds United Football Club was guaranteed promotion after sixteen years outside English football's elite and their fans were celebrating for all they were worth, completely oblivious to the needs of social distancing.

The supporters caught sight of the Leeds players up there in the stadium, partying as ecstatically as they were.

'We are Premier League, say we are Premier League!'

Exactly how did Leeds United recover their former status, how did they lose it way back when and how did they recover from almost going out of business?

This is the story of a football club that believed its hype, lost its way, gambled and failed – disastrously! This is the story of a football club that never lost its heart, but nearly lost its soul, ravaged and savaged by men who really should have known better. This is the story of not only how not to run a football club but also how to do so successfully.

Marching On Together!

'We've been through it all together, And we've had our ups and downs, We're gonna stay with you forever, At least until the world stops going round.'

CHAPTER ONE

Living the Dream

It took years to drag Leeds United Football Club kicking and screaming into the bright new commercial reality of football. Even after winning the league championship in 1992, the final season before the establishment of the Premier League, the club struggled to secure its share of the emerging riches.

That all changed in 1996 when Leeds United was taken over by Caspian Group plc and set off on a journey to the stars – by March 2001, the job appeared to be complete.

In both business and football terms, Leeds United was a glowing success. One of the most exciting teams in the Premier League was through to the last eight of the Champions League and commercially things were on the up.

Leeds United plc published impressive financial results. Total turnover soared to £57.1 million, with the figure set to rise to £86.3 million in the Champions League season. For a third successive year, the club was in the black.

Such financial success was unheard of for Leeds United. Historically, the club had depended on the largesse of local worthies, but it was becoming a bona fide commercial success.

Building a team capable of winning silverware would require major investment in the transfer market and in the autumn of 2000 chairman Peter Ridsdale and the United board pushed the boat out. They sanctioned the purchases of Olivier Dacourt, Mark Viduka and Dominic Matteo at a combined cost of £17.5 million. At a stroke, the three transfers catapulted Leeds into the big league. In November, they went even further, paying West Ham a British record £18 million for Rio Ferdinand and then adding Irish striker Robbie Keane, an initial loan deal being made permanent in May at a cost of £12 million.

Ridsdale and manager David O'Leary made a confident, capable and cohesive partnership, earning plaudits from the media for Leeds' progress. When they sat down in the summer to discuss their plans, O'Leary singled out Ferdinand as his number one target. Ridsdale was only too ready to do the deal.

Football-wise, the investment appeared sound. The team was on the rise and many thought Leeds were on the verge of overtaking Manchester United as England's leading side.

Certainly, that was O'Leary's ambition as he led Leeds with some assurance across the fields of Europe. His success prompted the board to reward him with a new six-year contract.

'I don't think we should accept that Man United are going to be up there for ever,' said Ridsdale. 'Somebody else's turn is coming.'

Ridsdale acknowledged football's financial realities and the widening gap between the haves and the have-nots. 'The time is fast approaching when the sort of wages we are talking about will not be sustainable by more than the odd club or two,' he warned. Leeds could only attract the calibre of player O'Leary coveted and afford the salaries and transfer fees involved if the club was successful. It was geared to European football and unless it qualified for Europe year in, year out, the board would have to take appropriate action, meaning cuts.

O'Leary had an embarrassment of riches at his disposal: in defence, goalkeeper Nigel Martyn behind a rearguard of Danny Mills, Ferdinand, Matteo and Ian Harte.

'England, England's Number One,' Elland Road would sing to Martyn as he established himself as the best Leeds keeper ever. He would always be the bridesmaid in the eyes of a succession of England managers, fated to be permanent back-up to David Seaman.

His storming runs down the right flank prompted chants that 'Danny Mills is F***ing Brilliant' while Harte was a constant threat from dead ball situations.

Across midfield, O'Leary would go with Lee Bowyer, Dacourt, David Batty and Harry Kewell while Viduka and either Keane or Alan Smith led the line.

It was a gifted set of individuals, internationals one and all, but it was as a collective that they really came into their own, a hard-running force of nature. Some of the players they faced in the Champions League had higher profiles, but Leeds had proven themselves able to live with the best, eliminating Barcelona, and pushing Milan and Lazio to the limit.

At home, only Manchester United were unquestionably superior and Leeds were mixing it successfully with Arsenal, Liverpool and Chelsea. The astonishing 4-3 defeat of Liverpool in November courtesy of four goals from Viduka and a 2-1 victory in the return at Anfield were highlights of an extraordinary campaign.

On 4 April 2001, as the season moved rapidly towards its climax, Leeds faced Deportivo La Coruna in the first leg of the Champions League quarter-final at Elland Road.

Deportivo midfielder Victor branded Leeds the weakest team left in the competition.

'We've heard a lot of talk like that,' said Ferdinand calmly in his pre-match press conference. 'But results speak more loudly than people.' His words epitomised the growing confidence in the Leeds camp.

Deportivo arrived at Elland Road with a reputation for a passing game and in the opening minutes they underlined their quality as they stroked the ball around. They threatened early but from the moment Harte cracked in a swerving drive from 25 yards which Francisco Molina spilled before claiming at the second attempt, it was all Leeds.

Harte sent a 40-yard cross-field ball to Bowyer, just inside the area. The twenty-four-year-old should have added to his tally of six goals in the competition. His clever touch saw him evade defender Cesar, but Molina raced out to block.

The Spaniards were rattled and Emerson was booked for a foul on Dacourt.

Viduka and Smith stoked up the pressure, muscling and hustling their way round the Spaniards. Smith's determination not to relinquish the ball on the edge of the area led to the opening goal after twenty-four minutes when Cesar conceded a free kick as he wrestled him to the floor. Harte whipped a vicious left foot thunderbolt into the net from the dead ball.

Leeds never looked back as they tore up the Yorkshire turf, with Kewell a constant threat down the left. In an early show of outstanding close control, he slipped past one defender, jinked around another and was unlucky to slice his final shot narrowly over from the tightest of angles. And Dacourt was rampant in midfield, snapping up the loose ball and unleashing a series of sweeping passes. Both players were involved in Leeds' second goal, five minutes into the second half.

The score had the best of Leeds stamped all over it. Viduka hassled the ball from a defender, allowing Smith to fire a raking right foot shot at goal. Molina tipped the effort round the post but Leeds profited from the corner. Kewell's cross found the head of Smith and the twenty-one-year-old buried the ball for his fifteenth goal of the season, his seventh in Europe.

Deportivo failed to make anything resembling a goal-scoring chance until the fifty-fifth minute when Makaay presented Martyn with an easy save. If Deportivo hoped that might signal a revival, they were wrong – Leeds cranked up the pace and Ferdinand powered home a third goal on the hour. He could not have chosen a better moment to score his first Leeds goal.

Kewell and Harte worked space from a corner and when second-half sub Valeron could only flick Kewell's cross on to the back post, Ferdinand plunged to nod home his first goal in four years.

Substitutes Tristan and Walter Pandiani almost snatched goals in injury-time, but Leeds held on for a vital clean sheet. Martyn had one nasty moment when he spilled a free kick but Matteo stepped in to clear. It was a fortunate break but you make your own luck in football and Leeds deserved it by the bucketload.

In the second leg in Spain a fortnight later, Deportivo were a different proposition. Kewell gave away a penalty early on when he nudged Victor off his feet as a cross came over. Djalminha coolly sent Martyn the wrong way from the spot. Tristan added a second after seventy-three minutes to leave Leeds desperately hanging on for twenty minutes before securing their place in the final four.

In between legs, Leeds beat Southampton and then won at Anfield to strengthen their Premier League challenge. Victories against West Ham and Chelsea kept the pot boiling, although Manchester United and Arsenal had cornered two of the three Champions League placings. Leeds were battling it out with Ipswich and Liverpool for the remaining spot.

Just at the wrong moment, Leeds' stamina gave way. They could only draw 0-0 with Valencia in the first leg of the Champions League semi-final and then lost to Arsenal at Highbury.

A disastrous seven days ended with a 3-0 defeat at Valencia. The Spaniards were too strong for a weary Leeds team, who ended the game with ten men after Smith was dismissed for a dangerous tackle.

O'Leary paid tribute to his players for reaching the last four and was magnanimous in defeat, praising Valencia for their performance. He had to contend with the bitter disappointment of missing out to Liverpool in the chase for a Champions League spot, with Leeds condemned to the less lucrative climes of the UEFA Cup. The failure would have far-reaching consequences in the years to come.

CHAPTER TWO

The Cracks Begin to Show

The slow summer months of 2001 brought the customary glut of back-page gossip about player movement for Leeds. There were rumours that fringe players like Jason Wilcox were on the way out of Elland Road but there was no concrete news.

Peter Ridsdale promised fans that things were moving with 'the club's wanted list' but would give no idea of the timescale. 'Sometimes it takes a lot of patience to get the right players, as we demonstrated with Rio Ferdinand,' he said. 'All I can say is that there is a lot of work that has been going on behind the scenes and that we will continue to be patient until we get the players David O'Leary wants.'

In the eventuality, United declined to bring in any new players, O'Leary declaring his confidence in the first-team pool. He insisted that the priority had been instead to tie down the existing squad to longer-term deals and commended Ridsdale on his progress in that regard.

Leeds' valuation of Mark Viduka did not deter Real Madrid and journalists from Madrid newspaper *La Marca* agitated, printing up a Madrid shirt with 'Viduka 9' on the back and trying to get him to pose with it. Viduka apologised to O'Leary and denied his agent's claims. 'He is not representing me in any way,' he said. 'I don't know anything about Real Madrid and I want to make it clear I am happy at Leeds. I want to stay at the club and win trophies.'

United's strategy seemed to make sense – tie down the big jewels to long-term contracts on increased salaries – but it was stoking up trouble for the future, increasing the importance of qualifying for the Champions League.

O'Leary impressed upon the players the need to 'start putting things on the sideboard' and live up to the expectations growing around the club.

The Cracks Begin to Show

The Irishman accepted that Europe's premier competition was a must and 'I won't need to be sacked if I'm doing badly.'

This would be a crucial season for Leeds United in many ways, testing the club's ability to sustain the progress made over the previous three years.

Leeds answered the Irishman's call to arms when the action began, their performances brutally effective if far from easy on the eye.

In a gritty clash with Arsenal at Highbury, referee Jeff Winter red-carded Danny Mills and Lee Bowyer and dished out cautions to Eirik Bakke, Viduka and Olly Dacourt. Leeds etched out a 2-1 victory courtesy of goals from Ian Harte and Viduka.

An unbeaten eleven-game opening burst with just five goals conceded took Leeds to the head of the Premiership table. Draws with Liverpool, Chelsea and Manchester United were ticked off to add to victory at Arsenal.

Yet, while things looked good, there were issues behind the scenes. The club's value on the stock market slumped to £36 million, much to Ridsdale's frustration. His Canute-like pleas to reverse the trend betrayed his naïvety. The market quailed at the size of United's debt, estimated at £50 million. Ridsdale's solution to the problems was two-pronged: reduce the liability by way of a bond issue and enhance matchday income with a new 60,000-capacity stadium. When Ridsdale put the question to the season ticket-holders and members of the supporters' club, there was overwhelming support for a new ground. The sale of naming rights would fill the coffers, insisted Ridsdale, but he didn't put that to the vote.

Disregarding his confidence of the summer and the club's tight finances, O'Leary bolstered the squad. He splashed £18 million to bring in Derby midfielder Seth Johnson and Liverpool and England goal poacher Robbie Fowler. A spiky O'Leary rubbished claims that he had spent £100 million on players since his appointment, insisting that the net spend 'was more like £60 million'. With Leeds also pursuing Nottingham Forest's Jermaine Jenas and Feyenoord's Australian international Brett Emerton, there was a sharp intake of breath at what many considered a high-risk strategy.

Why spend millions on an average player like Johnson when you have internationals such as Dacourt, Bowyer, Bakke, Kewell, Wilcox, Batty and McPhail available to you? With strikers like Viduka, Smith and Keane and a recovering Bridges, how could you squeeze in Fowler?

Ridsdale scoffed at the criticism and pressed ahead with a twenty-five-year bond scheme in September. The club borrowed £60 million from the City to refinance the substantial short-term debt, adding to the £21.3 million owed in financing the big transfers. The board had gambled the club's entire future on a headlong dash for the Champions League.

The final damaging poke in the ribs came when a long-running legal case concluded.

In January 2000, Lee Bowyer and Jonathan Woodgate were implicated in the beating of Sarfraz Najeib, a young Asian student, after a drunken evening in Leeds city centre.

Bowyer was found not guilty on all counts, although the judge accused him of attempting to mislead the jury and ordered that he stood legal costs of £1 million.

Woodgate was not so lucky, convicted of causing affray and sentenced to one hundred hours' community service. His friend, Paul Clifford, was sentenced to six years in jail for his leading role in the assault and another, Neale Caveney, was found guilty of affray. He also had to find his own legal costs of £1 million.

At that point the positive propaganda pouring out of Ridsdale's office began to unravel. Bowyer and Woodgate were slaughtered in the media while O'Leary's book, *Leeds United on Trial*, was panned for capitalising on the episode. O'Leary escaped a charge of bringing the game into disrepute but his holier-than-thou attitude caused ructions at Elland Road as he slated Bowyer and Woodgate for their lies and lack of discipline.

The mutual admiration society of O'Leary and Ridsdale crumbled under pressure from the media, with the chairman claiming that several players had told him they were on the verge of refusing to play for the manager.

The relationship between Ridsdale and Bowyer was every bit as fraught, the midfielder transfer-listed after refusing to pay a £64,000 fine for being drunk on the night of the assault. The black sheep was welcomed back after agreeing to pay the fine, but he did so resentfully. The damage had been done and Ridsdale deepened the wound when he told BBC Radio 5 Live that with the benefit of hindsight, he would not have signed Bowyer.

Whether it was down to such distractions or nothing more complicated than a loss of form, United's results nosedived. Three successive wins with clean sheets immediately after Christmas cemented Leeds' leadership of the Premiership, but then the rot set in.

Following a fractious FA Cup defeat at third-tier Cardiff, Leeds lost nine games in a row, dropping to sixth in the Premiership and being eliminated from the UEFA Cup by PSV.

The chances of making it back into the money-spinning Champions League looked slim and the boardroom was gripped by anxiety and recrimination.

In March, Ridsdale revealed that the club had made a loss of £13.8 million. If Leeds failed to qualify for the Champions League, he added, £30 million would have to be raised from player sales to reduce the debt (said to be more than £85 million). The club had the squad independently valued at £198 million but the City priced the entire club at just £25 million.

The Cracks Begin to Show

Explaining the loss, Ridsdale blamed the uncertainty surrounding the Woodgate-Bowyer trial. Injuries to Lucas Radebe and Michael Bridges had forced Leeds to carry more players on their wage bill than they had wanted.

Ridsdale denied that plans for a new stadium were impacted by the financial problems. 'We're in discussions with three multinationals over naming rights and already have one indicative offer.'

Stories began circulating at the start of the year that O'Leary had lost it, his attitude to the players causing unrest. He complained about the depth and quality of his squad, slamming some players for their lack of discipline on the pitch, his ire focused on Smith and Mills.

After Smith was dismissed at Villa Park in November, O'Leary took him to task in an hour-long meeting. He warned in no uncertain terms that he would be transfer-listed if he could not control his temper. The red card shown to the player for elbowing Villa defender Alpay was the fifth of his career.

In unguarded moments, players could be heard criticising O'Leary. One player wondered out loud what would happen if he were to 'do what everyone at training wants and tw*t him'. The reputation of the 'big-headed c***' was in ruins.

O'Leary's serial stockpiling of big names suggested to the existing squad that he didn't consider them good enough. It also smacked of self-delusion given Ridsdale's warning that such overinvestment demanded Champions League qualification.

When some fans questioned his approach, O'Leary went on the offensive, biting the hands that fed him. His irritable outbursts were ill-advised, making matters worse with both supporters and the media.

The final straw came for Ridsdale and the board when O'Leary criticised them for their readiness to listen to offers for Rio Ferdinand. 'I don't want him to go but it's down to the plc.' O'Leary added insult to injury when he asked for a further £23 million to bring in three new players.

Driven to distraction by O'Leary's unwillingness to accept the reality of the finances, Ridsdale and the board sacked the Irishman on 27 June, plunging the club back into newspaper headlines of the worst sort as the press focused on a club in crisis.

Ridsdale declared his preference for manager as Celtic's Martin O'Neill, as he had before appointing O'Leary in 1998, but it became evident there was minimal chance of prising him away from Parkhead.

Ridsdale's attention shifted to Steve McClaren of Middlesbrough, who indicated his openness to a four-year contract. To exploit a get-out clause in McClaren's contract would have cost Leeds around £1 million at a time when they were under intense pressure to save money. As they pondered what to do, McClaren's close links with Manchester United gave some of the board cold feet and there was a sudden change of heart. They informed McClaren that their attention had switched to Terry Venables, former manager of Barcelona, Tottenham and England.

Venables was effectively third choice for the job, but Ridsdale enthused over the appointment of a 'special' coach who he felt could do for Leeds what Sir Bobby Robson had done at Newcastle. Ridsdale insisted that Leeds had 'got the right man to take the club forward'. There had been many names in the frame said the chairman, before insisting that Venables was 'the best coach and manager in the game'.

El Tel was given a two-year contract, with the option of a further two years. The £2 million salary was second only to that of Sir Alex Ferguson.

'The whole business had been conducted like a whirlwind,' said Venables. 'It was irresistible.' He received a call from Leeds to his home in Spain, Ridsdale came out to see him the next day and after two hours of talks a contract was agreed.

Asked about transfer rumours, Venables said he had not yet spoken to Rio Ferdinand but thought he could persuade him to stay at Elland Road. He added that it was down to Lee Bowyer whether he wanted to stay or not but he expected Jonathan Woodgate to be around for the long term.

Venables admitted that he might not be able to hold on to all of O'Leary's squad. 'We know that if we could, we'd like to keep them all, but the reality is we have to deal with certain situations. Peter has mentioned there is £15 million to be found and I took the job on that understanding. We will do whatever we can to satisfy that side of it.'

CHAPTER THREE

The Mighty Fall

Despite the promises that Rio Ferdinand was going nowhere, money talked. When Sir Alex Ferguson mentioned a fee of £30 million, there was no way that the Leeds board could say no. With problems so deep-rooted, they had little choice.

Ridsdale was adamant that he did not want to sell Ferdinand but was given little choice when the player submitted a transfer request, going on to stress that Manchester United was the only club he was interested in speaking to.

Ferdinand admitted that he would have gone public to force a move had he needed to. After sitting for five or six hours in the chairman's office, Ferdinand got his way and the move of his dreams.

Ridsdale rapidly rewrote history by claiming that Leeds had only signed Ferdinand as an insurance policy, because of uncertainty over Woodgate's future. He said that Leeds had an embarrassment of defensive riches and denied that Ferdinand was the pick. 'We have made a healthy profit on a player we only bought as cover in the first place.'

Few gave any credence to such a shallow and ill-conceived attempt at self-justification.

Other big deals were mooted involving Lee Bowyer, Gary Kelly, Olly Dacourt and Nigel Martyn, but the only departure was Robbie Keane to Spurs for £7 million.

With every sign that O'Leary's team was about to fall apart, the mood of the fans was not positive and the appointment of Terry Venables divided opinion. His reputation as a coach suggested to some that he might get the best out of an expensive squad – others derided him as an outsider with his best days behind him and whose questionable business ventures made him an unsuitable choice.

For one so experienced, Venables was guilty of some crass errors of judgement in his first few weeks in the job. That they so badly impacted the team spirit that O'Leary had left in tatters made them particularly unforgivable.

Venables led the squad on a pre-season tour of the Far East and Australia. Nigel Martyn, weary after spending the summer at the World Cup with England, chose not to travel. David Batty's fear of flying led him to also opt out. Consequently, Venables wrote both men out of his plans, instantly disenfranchising them and a large element of the fans for whom the pair were favourites.

He decided Batty had no more to give and cast him aside, exiling him to train with the reserves. It was not the wisest of moves. Batty threatened a lawsuit when Ridsdale claimed at the club's AGM that he was unfit.

Rumours of an £11 million bid from Juventus for Dacourt petered out and the Frenchman rejected a move to Lazio because of the fascist reputation of their supporters. Dacourt, his relationship with Venables irrevocably soured, was dropped. The pair had a very public falling out that led to Venables saying he was prepared to drive Dacourt to Italy himself in order to secure a deal with Roma.

Fowler suffered a recurrence of the hip injury that put paid to his World Cup campaign. An operation meant Leeds would not see the striker play until the end of November.

Venables' decision to indulge Kewell's desire to play up front was another critical error. It spread the perception among the squad that Kewell could twist Venables round his little finger. Viduka shed light on the atmosphere in the dressing room when he revealed that his international teammate had not spoken to him for two years.

There was endless chatter about the players Venables would bring in. Expectancy was high and there seemed to be new rumours every day of big deals. The club found enough money for Venables to sign Nick Barmby and Paul Okon and bring in Swedish defender Teddy Lucic on loan, but that was an uninspiring trio. Venables' preference for a one-paced Australian veteran over Dacourt and Batty was bizarre, given that they had so recently proved their quality during the Champions League campaign.

The Leeds United faithful started to rumble and grumble as days went by with no news and the perception grew that the squad was dysfunctional and lopsided. Nevertheless, there was a crowd of 40,000-plus for the opening game, as Manchester City visited Elland Road.

A successful promotion campaign under former England boss Kevin Keegan had instilled confidence in City, who gave Leeds a number of problems with Ali Benarbia, Eyal Berkovic and Nicolas Anelka all impressing. City hit the woodwork twice and had several good chances, but it was Leeds who struck first. New boy Barmby opened the scoring after fifteen minutes, stealing in on a deep cross from Bowyer to force the ball home from close in.

On the stroke of half-time, Barmby played Viduka into the clear and he finished clinically. Keane came off the bench to replace the Aussie after seventy minutes and ten minutes later he wrapped matters up after breaking clear. He exhibited outstanding presence of mind to chip the ball over the advancing keeper for one of the most spectacular finishes of the opening day.

A week later, Leeds faced another of the promoted sides. They held West Bromwich Albion at bay in a difficult opening half-hour as the Midlanders pressed them back. Leeds' finishing power was too much for an Albion side tipped from the start for relegation and six minutes before half-time Kewell side-footed home a cross from Mills.

After that, there was little doubt who would be the victors and in the fifty-second minute Bowyer curled home a shot from range. Viduka rounded the keeper after seventy minutes to tap in a third and even though Lee Marshall claimed a consolation goal in the closing seconds, Leeds ended easy victors.

The optimism was rudely dispelled with a 1-0 defeat at home to struggling Sunderland. Tellingly, the game brought Sunderland's first goal and points of the season. Fans who had been quick to laud Venables' attacking approach booed the team off the pitch. There was no relief at Birmingham days later when Leeds came away pointless from a trip to the third promoted side.

When the expected big money arrivals failed to materialise, the fans wanted to know what had happened to the treasure trove generated by Ferdinand's departure. While it appeared that there was money to rebuild, the fans grudgingly accepted the sale as good business, but now it was apparent that the bargain basement was the only store in town. This was no brave new world.

The mood around Elland Road was noticeably lighter than during the final six months of O'Leary's time, but there were few signs that Venables was the Messiah who could rescue a club on the downward curve.

The new man said from the off that he needed time to work with his players on the training pitch to get them playing his way, but the first real opportunity he had to work one-on-one with them coincided with an international break. His frustration was evident as international call-ups robbed him of two-thirds of his first team.

Smith and Bowyer were two of the missing men, on their way to memorable performances for England against Portugal. Smith scored his first international goal with a remarkable diving header from a pass by Bowyer, making his long-delayed debut.

The pair took their good form into their next club game, at Newcastle as Leeds pulled off one of the outstanding results of the opening weeks. Five minutes in, Kewell broke clear on the left and crossed for Viduka to open the scoring. Defenders vainly appealed that Kewell had been offside, but the fault was more with their slack marking than the assistant referee.

Paul Robinson demonstrated the form that had seen him promoted to the England bench with a succession of saves. Jonathan Woodgate, who had also returned to the international fold against Portugal, was another star performer as Leeds gave ample proof of their defensive resilience.

Three minutes from time, Smith crowned a wonderful personal week by blasting home a splendid second goal from the edge of the area.

The 2-0 score was flattering, but Venables' spirits were lifted, the victory setting up a huge fixture against Manchester United at Elland Road.

The fans took pains to make Ferdinand's first return trip an unpleasant one with chants of 'One greedy bastard', and he was booed every time he touched the ball. It was clear for all to see that Woodgate was in the better form of the two defenders.

It may have been one of the weakest Manchester midfields for years, but their quartet was still strong enough to outmanoeuvre Leeds in the first period, with Ryan Giggs given the time and space to dominate. Leeds were reprieved by Ruud van Nistelrooy's lack of sharpness, and they were relieved to be still level at the interval.

Venables shook things up, recognising that Viduka and Kewell were off the pace. He brought Radebe on for the injured Matteo, but the key change was Bakke for the ineffectual Barmby. He pulled Kewell back into midfield and instructed Smith and Bowyer to push further forward to support Viduka.

The changes had the desired effect. Leeds were brighter, with Bowyer going close in the opening seconds. Bakke's physical presence made a significant difference, particularly after sixty-three minutes when he clashed with Butt, leading to the midfielder's withdrawal with a hip injury. Luke Chadwick replaced him, playing wide and allowing Beckham to move into a central role.

Within three minutes Leeds took the lead. Chadwick moved out to challenge Harte, 35 yards from goal, and showed him inside onto his supposedly weaker right foot. Harte calmly accepted the invitation and floated over a wonderful cross. Kewell rose unchallenged in the heart of the area to flick a clever header into the far corner.

It was the cue for exultant celebrations at the corner flag and triumphal cries of 'Rio, Rio, what's the score?'

Two such unexpected victories provided a fillip, and the early kick-off time meant that for a few hours at least, Leeds sat on top of the table, but that was the high point for Venables.

There was more good news when striker Michael Bridges, out of action with a bad injury for the best part of two years, returned to the bench for the UEFA Cup tie against Metalurh Zaporizhzhya. He came on to heartfelt

The Mighty Fall

applause after sixty-four minutes with Leeds struggling for a goal, and had a key role when Smith finally broke the deadlock.

It looked like the Ukrainians would escape with a priceless draw after a mean defensive display, but Bridges was a good luck charm. There were just ten minutes remaining when Leeds pierced the defensive rearguard. Harte pumped a ball forward and Bridges was onto it in a flash. He kept the ball in and turned it back into the path of Smith who fired home from 6 yards.

Leeds couldn't add to the goal but had crucially managed to keep a clean sheet. A late equaliser from Barmby saw Leeds through in the second leg.

Venables was less enamoured with events in the weeks that followed. Smith missed a penalty as Leeds went down by a single goal at Blackburn and were then on the wrong end of a resounding 4-1 drubbing at home to champions Arsenal.

Harte had been given a chasing by Keith Gillespie at Blackburn and was omitted against Arsenal, with Mills switched to left-back and Gary Kelly on the other flank. The changes left Leeds looking lopsided and out of sorts. The result flattered the Yorkshire side – Arsenal had won at a canter.

Leeds' stop-start campaign continued to stutter. Neither one of two poor sides could manage a goal when United visited Aston Villa on 6 October, and then Leeds lost at home to Liverpool. Twice Leeds took the lead at Middlesbrough, twice conceded an equaliser, and then saw Smith dismissed for a second bookable offence, harsh though the decision appeared. Everton won at Elland Road for the first time in more than fifty years when the youthful Wayne Rooney made Lucas Radebe look leaden-footed. Even worse, two goals in the closing seconds saw a Worthington Cup lead at First Division Sheffield United turned upside down and Leeds tumbling out of the competition at the first hurdle.

The first half-hearted cries of 'Venables Out' were heard on the terraces. 'It is frustrating, we are not getting the results that our play deserves,' said Venables.

The frowns were temporarily lifted by a gripping 4-3 win at West Ham, but Leeds had almost contrived to throw away a 4-1 half-time lead. West Ham, in the most appalling run of form, defended abysmally in the first half. They looked a different side after the break and enjoyed total dominance. United retreated into desperate defence, looking bemused and bewildered in the face of a sustained assault. Venables was on the edge of his seat throughout a terrible second half and breathed a sigh of relief at the end.

Mixed in with those stuttering performances came two UEFA Cup victories over Hapoel Tel Aviv. The away leg saw Smith turn in a virtuoso performance with all four goals in a sparkling 4-1 success. The Israelis had pilloried Smith after the first leg for his aggressive approach, but he now showed what a good player he was, earning praise from an exultant Venables.

Branded a 'foul-mouthed thug' and a 'provocateur' by Hapoel players in the build-up to the game, Smith for once played in his favoured striking role with Viduka absent and he revelled in the opportunity.

It was only a temporary relief for Venables as he suffered a string of dire results. Any faint hopes Leeds harboured of a decent season vanished during November and December as they lost four straight Premiership matches. The first was 4-2 at home to Bolton who came back strongly at the death. Leeds had the lead, before Bolton first equalised and then added two late goals to steal the points.

There were problems in the camp: no one could adequately explain what had happened to the most exciting young team in the Premiership. The loss of Ferdinand and Keane had been damaging, but Venables still had a strong squad, one good enough to beat Newcastle and Manchester United without conceding. However, he also had a dispirited group which could lose to Sunderland, Birmingham, Bolton and Sheffield United, and for which the clichéd phrase 'too good to go down' was far too positive.

The financial problems crystallised into a £33 million loss and overall debt of £77 million. Undeterred, Peter Ridsdale continued to campaign for a move to a new stadium. More corporate hospitality places would boost profits but planning issues meant a return to the drawing board as the focus switched to redeveloping Elland Road.

Leeds were shocked at the lack of interest when they sold the television rights for the UEFA Cup games. The Champions League had netted the Whites £4 million, but they received less than £150,000 for November's matches with Hapoel.

A considerable consolation came for Venables in this period with the emergence of James Milner. The Horsforth youngster was just sixteen years and 309 days when he came on against West Ham to become the second youngest player of the Premiership era. History was created when he scored in the 2-1 win at Sunderland on Boxing Day to break Wayne Rooney's record as the youngest Premiership goalscorer. Milner – eight days shy of his seventeenth birthday – beat Rooney by four days with his fiftieth-minute goal. He only had to wait two days to score his first home goal – a spectacular effort against Chelsea that left Marcel Desailly flat on his backside.

Milner took Bakke's pass in his stride, ran at Desailly and flummoxed the World Cup-winning colossus with two deft touches of his right foot before curling a beauty round Ed de Goey into the far corner of the net.

Venables' handling of Milner's precocious talent was crucial. He took care to shelter him from the media spotlight and reaped the rewards. Milner was normality itself in the dressing room, greatly impressing his more senior colleagues.

The Mighty Fall

A 2-0 defeat at Spurs fuelled the chants for Venables to go and UEFA Cup dismissal at the hands of Malaga amplified the cacophony.

Following calls for action, Ridsdale criticised Venables at the AGM, but he granted the manager more time. It seemed a sound decision when three wins over Christmas saw Leeds flirt with the top half of the table, but the improvement was short-lived. Points-wise their haul was a dismal four points from twenty-seven after a New Year's Day win over Birmingham.

The transfer window brought tensions boiling to the surface. Venables accepted that some players would have to be sold to reduce the debt but if he had known six internationals would be sold by the end of January, he would surely not have taken the job.

Bowyer ended a tumultuous two years with a move to West Ham for a nominal fee, Dacourt was loaned out to Roma and Fowler signed for Manchester City. The breakdown of Seth Johnson's move to Middlesbrough left the board under pressure to generate more cash and everything came to a head with the sale of Jonathan Woodgate.

Venables had been assured that the sale of Fowler meant Woodgate would stay, and he was genuinely shocked when on the last day of the transfer window the plc board accepted Newcastle's £9 million bid. Venables came within a whisker of walking out in disgust after seething through a tense press conference sat next to a down-mouthed Ridsdale.

A home defeat by Middlesbrough rendered Venables' position untenable and he was only too happy to call time on a disastrous stay at Elland Road. On 21 March, his contract was brought to an end by mutual consent.

CHAPTER FOUR
Cheer Up Peter Reid

One of Peter Ridsdale's final acts as chairman of Leeds United was appointing Peter Reid as caretaker following the dismissal of Venables. The announcement came just hours after the departure of El Tel.

Reid, sacked as Sunderland manager in October after seven years with the Wearsiders, was delighted to be back in football.

'I snapped Mr Ridsdale's hand off,' Reid told a press conference. 'I was just desperate to get back in.'

Scouser Reid, an old school football man, was one of the game's great characters. A BBC documentary of Sunderland's 1996/97 season caught Reid blurting out nineteen expletives in forty-five seconds. He was tearing into the players at half-time against Southampton as they battled against relegation. 'That's the way I am in the dressing room,' said Reid. 'It's the way I do my job.'

Reid ingratiated himself with United fans by announcing that he was happy to bring David Batty back into first-team contention. 'David is a fine player, I know that much. He is a very experienced hand and is exactly the kind of player that I like.'

Ten days later, Ridsdale fell on his sword as he confirmed disappointing financial results for the six months to December. Ridsdale talked about the pressures that had been brought to bear on him and his family following the fire sale of players. He would long be scapegoated for United's collapse and bore the brunt of supporters' anger. After five years as chairman, he was replaced by Professor John McKenzie, the club's biggest individual shareholder.

McKenzie owed his appointment to his experience in turning round distressed companies. He promised that further player sales would be 'a last resort … You cannot just cut away at the business and lose the quality it has or you lose everything. I would like a team capable of getting us back in European football next season.'

The scale of his task quickly became clear to Reid – defeat at Liverpool in his opening game saw Leeds slip to sixteenth.

The next match, on 5 April, offered no solace with a trip to meet Alan Curbishley's upwardly mobile Charlton at the Valley.

Reid kept faith for the most part with Venables' selection at Anfield, but now he dropped five players, including Venables' four recruits: Lucic, Raul Bravo, Okon and Barmby.

There was a freshness to Leeds' performance, coming down to something as simple as team spirit. Good old-fashioned determination shone through in a display which hearkened back to the days of United's glorious assault on the Champions League.

An inspired Alan Smith was instantly in Charlton faces. Almost single-handed, he tore the Addicks apart, giving a masterclass in how to mess up the opposition without resorting to violence.

So absolute was Leeds' command that it was fully nine minutes before Charlton got out of their own half and Leeds opened the scoring as the pressure told.

Harry Kewell found Mark Viduka, whose instant control allowed him to feed Smith. The blond striker angled the ball across the face of goal for Kewell, drifting in for a simple side-foot home.

Leeds added a second after thirty-four minutes with Smith again the architect. In the 18-yard area with his back to goal and Richard Rufus tight enough to share his shirt, Smith rolled his marker, prompting him to send the striker sprawling for a clear penalty.

Ian Harte and Viduka bickered testily over the spot kick before the Irishman snatched the ball and fired it home. An obviously furious Viduka gave Harte a roasting, continuing to show his displeasure even after the goal.

Three minutes from the interval, Smith was at it again, beating Rufus in the air and nodding the ball on for Viduka to chest down and drive home low from 20 yards.

Moments later, Charlton responded with Scott Parker storming into the area. Lucas Radebe's crude challenge made the penalty decision straightforward and Jason Euell gratefully converted with Charlton's first attempt of the day.

Coming on the stroke of half-time, the goal could have set nerves on edge but Leeds drew breath and bounced back. Eight minutes after the interval, Smith was away again to set up Viduka's second. The defence retreated in disarray before his run and he slipped the ball sideways to Viduka, who steered the ball home from the edge of the box.

The away support, bemused by the turn of affairs, broke into cries of 'What the f*** is going on?'

Smith was destined not to make it onto the scoresheet, but he had a hand in everything that was good about the performance. It was no surprise when he secured a second penalty after fifty-six minutes, slipping clear of Rufus to bear into the area only for Luke Young to send him flying.

Harte knew it would have been more than his life was worth to deprive Viduka a second time, and graciously withdrew, allowing the Australian to complete his hat-trick with a deft and impertinent chip after committing Kiely to the dive.

Viduka nearly crowned his contribution with a fourth when substitute Jason Wilcox played him clear in the middle, but his drive crashed back off the bar. Leeds were already 6-1 up, the predatory instincts of Kewell bringing an interception, a sprint through the left channel and a curled shot into the net.

Few teams could have lived with Leeds on the day. Reid gushed over the quality of the all-round display, which saw Leeds rise to fourteenth with a six-point cushion over the relegation zone. 'The catalyst for our win was the work ethic. The players let their football do all the talking.'

The triumph was followed by an ill-deserved 2-2 draw at home to Tottenham, while only two goals in the final ten minutes at Southampton gave a semblance of competitiveness to a drab 3-2 defeat. A brace from Viduka beat Fulham to ease fears of the drop, but Leeds squandered a twenty-first-minute lead against Blackburn to slump to another defeat. Coupled with Bolton's battling draw with Arsenal and West Ham's spirited victory at Manchester City, the result left United sixteenth, one point above Wanderers and three above the Hammers. The final relegation spot rested between the three teams with two games left.

The form of Bolton and West Ham was cause for concern and the first of Leeds' two remaining games was a daunting one, away to reigning champions Arsenal.

The game was set for Sunday 4 May, with Leeds' relegation rivals having the opportunity to turn the screw in their Saturday fixtures.

The Hammers were first into action, facing Chelsea at Upton Park. The Blues were playing for a place in the Champions League but West Ham secured the points with a late goal from Paolo Di Canio. It took them ahead of Bolton and level on points with Leeds.

Bolton, away to FA Cup finalists Southampton in an evening kick-off, settled for a goalless stalemate which left them on forty-one points, level with their rivals and splitting them on goal difference.

Reid sought to make his side difficult to beat at Highbury with a 4-4-1-1 formation, though a draw at Highbury would have been of little value.

Arsenal had been suffering their own stutter in the Premiership and their weakened side, missing Lauren and Sol Campbell at the back and Patrick Vieira in their engine room, started apprehensively.

Leeds took immediate advantage when Wilcox launched a punt upfield towards Kewell. The veteran pairing of Oleg Luzhny and Martin Keown simply couldn't get close to the Australian as he collected the ball and lashed home a glorious left-footed curler from 25 yards. David Seaman never came near to seeing it, let alone keeping it out.

Arsenal began to find their form and after thirty minutes midfielder Ray Parlour fired in a shot from outside the area which reared up on the bounce, forcing Robinson into a fingertip save onto the bar. As it dropped back into play, Thierry Henry was in the right place at the right home to head the equaliser.

Parlour had another long-range effort which Duberry blocked on the line. Wiltord thought he had scored when he followed in to force home the ball after Henry hit the post, but an offside flag told him otherwise.

The interval came at just the right time for Leeds, disrupting the Gunners' rhythm, and United struck even more quickly in the second half than they had the first.

With three minutes gone, Ashley Cole was penalised and Ian Harte stepped up to take the free kick from 20 yards out. He had scored from trademark free kicks for two years running in the fixture, but Arsenal were either not concentrating, or judged that the ball was too far out, for their wall contained just two men. The Irishman needed no more bidding and looped over a great strike which was deflected past Seaman at the far post.

Arsenal regained the initiative, relocating their unstoppable form of the autumn. They had Leeds on the ropes for long stretches and fashioned a second equaliser just after the hour. Henry freed Robert Pires on the left and he drove into the penalty area, turning away from Danny Mills. Dennis Bergkamp took the cut back to thrash eagerly into the roof of the net from close in.

Bergkamp nearly added a second but his curled effort drifted wide, and then Henry struck the foot of the post. Leeds were on the ropes and Kanu, coming on for Toure, added to the mayhem, but Arsenal grew anxious as they saw their Premiership chances drifting away.

Despite some frenetic attacking, Arsenal were looking less and less likely to score, as Leeds seemed willing to settle for a draw. Arsene Wenger's tinkering in search of a breakthrough was ultimately his side's undoing.

Bergkamp now laboured in a passive midfield while substitute Jermaine Pennant was starved of the ball when introduced wide on the right. After eighty-eight minutes his eagerness to show what he could do saw him surrender possession. Matteo seized on the opportunity to set Leeds quickly onto a raking counter-attack with a long ball to Viduka.

It looked ominously like offside, but the Aussie did not wait for the whistle and killed the ball instinctively. His clever drag back through his own legs wrong-footed the static Luzhny and gave him space. He coolly steadied himself and swerved the ball unerringly round Seaman and in at the far corner to settle the contest and preserve Leeds' Premiership status.

Five days after the Highbury triumph, Reid's appointment was made permanent on a rolling one-year contract. His basic package of £500,000 per annum would rise to £1 million if Leeds regained a European place.

Reid's first act was to dispense with the services of assistant manager Eddie Gray and head coach Brian Kidd. Few tears were shed over the departure of ex-Manchester United man Kidd, whom many amongst the Elland Road faithful blamed for the collapse in the club's fortunes. Gray, however, was a different case, and his forty-year association with the club made him a fans' favourite.

Unconcerned with any potential loss of popularity, Reid quickly brought in Kevin Blackwell, who had worked under Neil Warnock at First Division Sheffield United.

Teddy Lucic and Raul Bravo returned to their parent clubs, while Paul Okon was released from his contract, moving back to Italy with Serie B side Vicenza. Olly Dacourt made his loan move to Roma permanent in a protracted £3.5 million deal.

Paul Robinson was on the verge of a reunion with David O'Leary, now in the hot seat at Aston Villa, but the deal broke down over the keeper's personal terms after a £3.25 million fee was agreed.

The summer's one major departure was surrounded with controversy.

When it became clear that Harry Kewell had decided his future lay away from Elland Road, Professor McKenzie accepted the inevitable and sanctioned a move, eager to avoid Kewell leaving on a Bosman free transfer when his contract expired in 2004.

The chairman was outfoxed by Kewell and his agent, Bernie Mandic, who engineered a move to Liverpool. Leeds could have got more money by selling Kewell to Chelsea, Manchester United or Barcelona, but the winger would have none of it and Mandic reminded Leeds with a huge grin that Kewell could sit out the remaining twelve months of his contract and then move for nothing.

On 9 July, the United board accepted a £5 million offer from Anfield but banked just half of the sum. Mandic took £2 million, while the remaining £500,000 was paid into Kewell's employee benefit trust.

McKenzie was branded naïve in the extreme as United saw another prize asset walk away for a fraction of his true worth.

Delays in sorting out Kewell's deal meant that four experienced Premiership players slipped through Reid's fingers as he sought to replenish his squad. Deals had been worked out for Liverpool's Patrik Berger and Markus Babbel but they chose instead to join Portsmouth and Blackburn, while Henning Berg swapped Ewood Park for Rangers and Paolo Di Canio abandoned West Ham for Charlton. Reid was devastated when the moves collapsed, forced to hastily seek out alternatives.

Reid recruited a number of players on loans, and took another, Chelsea schemer Jody Morris, on a free transfer.

The most notable signing was winger Jermaine Pennant, who had shown enough promise with Notts County when he was just fifteen to persuade Arsenal to sign him for £2 million. He was the only newcomer that made a contribution worthy of the name.

French League players Didier Domi, Lamine Sakho, Zoumana Camara, Cyril Chapuis and Salomon Olembe all signed twelve-month loan agreements, as did Brazilian World Cup-winning defender Roque Junior, who had tasted Champions League success with Milan.

There were only fifteen players available for the first day of pre-season training and Blackwell warned Reid the squad wouldn't be good enough. The manager had been assured that money would be available to strengthen in August but it never appeared; the loan players arrived too late to be fully integrated. Youngsters were available but they were unproven and raw. The cupboard rang hollow.

The victory at Arsenal fooled no one. The heart had been torn out of O'Leary's side and a difficult season was anticipated.

A characteristically blunt Reid admitted he wasn't getting the best out of the players and that their attitude wasn't right. After a winless pre-season, he hoped that 'the competitive nature of the Premiership will bring the best out of them ... It's going to be a very difficult season, I'm under no illusions about that.'

His prediction proved sadly accurate. Leeds lost nine of their first thirteen games, sliding inexorably towards relegation.

The most disappointing loanee was the one with the biggest reputation, Roque Junior. The Brazilian's seven first-team appearances yielded four cautions, one dismissal, six defeats, twenty-four goals conceded and a horribly tarnished CV.

Kevin Blackwell admitted that bringing in six foreign players at one time was just too many. Just when the club needed to build team spirit, the arrivals disrupted the camp.

There was little cheer in the Carling Cup with Leeds owing survival in a second round tie against Swindon Town to goalkeeper Paul Robinson for an injury-time goal. The third-tier side worked themselves into a two-goal lead before Harte pulled a goal back with thirteen minutes remaining. As the game moved into stoppage time, Robinson came forward for a corner. He got his head to the ball and suddenly Leeds were level, going on to win the game on penalties.

Any hopes of a decent run were extinguished by a second-string Man United side in the next round. Roque Junior enjoyed a rare success with both goals in a 3-2 defeat, marking the moment with a manic conga of celebration.

David Batty showed that he could still make a telling contribution with a string of man of the match performances. He was a rare breed, with Matteo and the heroic Smith, in escaping the condemnation of the fans. Reid was effusive with his praise for the former England midfielder.

The defeat to Man United was the third in a row and four days later pace-setters Arsenal won 4-1 at Elland Road to leave Leeds second bottom after their worst start to a season since 1981. There was huge speculation about Reid's position. McKenzie and deputy chairman Allan Leighton failed to reach a decision on the manager's future at a breakfast meeting in London. McKenzie travelled back for a heart-to-heart with Reid in a Halifax hotel and discussed severance pay. The chairman left the meeting saying that he would sleep on it.

McKenzie was swayed by a phone call to John Boocock, chairman of the Leeds United Independent Supporters' Association.

Boocock was shocked to receive the call, but left McKenzie in no doubt as to who was to blame for the team's free-fall. 'I'm just flabbergasted at the situation,' said Boocock. 'I can't see any great movement from the supporters towards calling for Reid's head. He has to be given more time. It is the players that the fans are angry with — not Reid.'

Giving Reid the dreaded vote of confidence, McKenzie insisted that the pair's relationship was healthy but refused to say how long Reid had been given.

Leeds were dumped into bottom spot by Leicester's victory over fellow strugglers Blackburn on 2 November but Reid hoped to end the slump with a trip to mid-table Portsmouth. The game looked relatively straightforward after a challenging run of fixtures against Liverpool, Manchester United and Arsenal.

Leeds travelled to Fratton Park without Mark Viduka after a spat between Reid and the player.

Problems between the two began in the summer after referee Alan Kaye told Reid to substitute Viduka against York to escape a dismissal eight minutes into the game. Reid brought the Aussie off again during a subsequent defeat at Burnley.

When Viduka asked for a transfer, Reid warned him that he would get a move only if he tabled a written request, which would mean forfeiting any money still outstanding from his £1 million-plus signing-on fee. The two men had a stand-up row in front of the other players.

The row seemed to have blown over until Viduka arrived late for the game with Arsenal and was unceremoniously dropped.

Punctuality had never been one of the striker's virtues. During his first season at Leeds, he was more than once late for training, his timekeeping driving O'Leary mad. 'It shows a lack of respect for the rest of the people here,' said the Irishman.

When Viduka also turned up late for Friday's training session, there was a further argument with Reid. Viduka stormed off, telling his teammates, 'If you want to go down, stick with this fella.' Reid, beside himself with rage, dropped Viduka from his travelling party and fined him a week's wages – £65,000.

Out from the surrender to Arsenal went Camara, Bridges, Sakho and the injured Batty. Among their replacements was Jody Morris, on police bail while rape allegations were investigated. When the news came through that Reid had chosen to field Roque Junior in an unfamiliar midfield role, there were jeers of 'You don't know what you're doing.'

Sadly, they were absolutely right. Leeds finished on the wrong end of a 6-1 defeat, the club's heaviest since 1959. There had been no fight, no spirit, nothing – some of the players had simply given up. A forlorn Reid admitted as much, saying there was no desire to play football. 'At the age of 47, I'm not going to start resigning now. I have to get on with it. That second half was the worst forty-five minutes of my managerial career and the players don't deserve to pick up their wage packets … The white flag ran up so early it was untrue.'

The directors had seen enough and Reid was gone within days, though he had nothing but praise for the club, describing his time at Leeds as an honour and privilege.

'Whoever the next manager is, they must be given time to do the job. It could take years, not months, for Leeds United to turn around and the club needs stability. Everyone has to pull together from top to bottom. That will be the key for the club in the future. If everyone does that, I'm sure Leeds will come through this.'

CHAPTER FIVE
Club for Sale

The autumn of 2003 saw Leeds United in a desperate race against time on two fronts. They needed points to stave off the looming threat of relegation while conjuring up enough cash to see them through a long, hard winter.

In terms of footballing matters, Professor McKenzie turned to club legend Eddie Gray, who had been with the club as a player and manager since 1965. He sought out someone just as eminent to deal with the business problems.

Trevor Birch had a track record in football finance, masterminding the rescue of Chelsea from a position almost as challenging as that now facing Leeds.

Chartered accountant Birch had been a decent footballer but retired at twenty-three to concentrate on a career in business. He joined Ernst & Young where he specialised in managing insolvencies. That was the combination of experience that prompted Chelsea to appoint him chief executive in 2002.

Ken Bates had famously bought Chelsea in 1982 for a pound and had planned to build a business empire by developing the Stamford Bridge stadium as a leisure and hotel complex. But his overweening ambition led to problems when he raised huge loans on the financial markets.

Meeting the massive repayments pushed Chelsea into a vicious downward cycle and Birch was brought in to find an escape route. He spent months unsuccessfully trying to restructure a £75 million Eurobond before accepting defeat and negotiating the £140 million sale of the club to Russian billionaire Roman Abramovich.

Leeds had been in the market for a chief executive for almost a year. Allan Leighton advised McKenzie to appoint Birch, who had walked away from Stamford Bridge after the sale to Abramovich. Birch took office as chief executive at Elland Road a week before the depressing defeat at Portsmouth in November. His first job was to put Reid out of his misery.

McKenzie conducted an urgent review of the club's financial position following his appointment in March and identified a programme of cost savings to return it to profitable trading. There were 'major changes in personnel', including the departure of Peter Ridsdale, chief operating officer Stephen Harrison and operations director David Spencer. 'Together with player wage savings from transfers earlier in the year,' boasted McKenzie, 'the resultant cost savings amount to nearly £20 million.'

Ridsdale seethed with self-righteous indignation, adamant that most of the improvements had been set in train before he quit. He berated McKenzie for hogging the credit while laying the sins of the world at his predecessor's doorstep. Ridsdale was adamant that there were other guilty men but the legend of the exorbitant expenditure on goldfish would dog him to the grave while the names of the other directors faded from memory.

While ongoing costs were set to fall, it would take time for the savings to come through fully and the club had to stand the cost in the meantime of paying people off. Sacking O'Leary, Venables and Reid resulted in severance costs of £6.5 million – Ridsdale, Harrison and Spencer drew £628,000 of their annual salaries of £780,000 in a year in which their pay-offs totalled £656,000.

£4.6 million of interest on the £60 million securitisation loan was paid on 1 September and the club was caught napping by the scale of the loss in income. McKenzie mocked Ridsdale for 'an unrealistic view of achievable income' as television and broadcasting fees fell by £12.3 million.

McKenzie concluded that the club needed a cash injection of £5 million to keep it going until the end of the season.

Payments were coming up over the next few weeks which Leeds simply didn't have the money to cover. Their options were limited – sell players in the January window or negotiate with the club's creditors for more time. Selling the crown jewels would almost guarantee relegation and Birch set his stall out against such a strategy. McKenzie and the board reported that if the creditors wouldn't play ball, then they might have to seek the protection of administration.

The main creditors were the bondholders for the £60 million loan, MetLife, Teachers and M&G. The loan had been secured against future ticket sales with relevant sums to be set aside in a separate bank account until they were paid over – at 30 June 2003, the sum in the 'locked box' was £8.1 million.

£21.3 million was owed to Gerling, the credit insurer of REFF, who provided United's player finance lease arrangements, and there was another £7.7 million due to HMRC.

Birch asked the bondholders to agree to a deferral of payments and allow the club to use £4 million from the locked box to cover its operating expenses while he looked for potential purchasers.

There were reports of a potential rescue deal involving Leighton and Sheikh Abdul Mubarak Al-Khalifa, a member of the Bahrain Royal family. The first phase of a complex restructuring of the debt had reached an advanced stage. Leighton's ARM Holdings had confirmed their intention to inject £4.4 million in cash as part of a rights issue of shares.

Birch's negotiations with the bondholders ran into difficulties at the end of November and the board was forced to abandon the planned rights issue.

An unholy row erupted when Birch asked the squad to help out by accepting a deferral of wages. Advised by the Professional Footballers' Association, the players asked for all other options to be considered first, including the sale of a player, the favoured option being Alan Smith to Newcastle.

Birch requested a deferral of between 30 and 35 per cent. The players accepted the idea in principle but the publicity surrounding a meeting with them and the subsequent criticism from fans exacerbated an already febrile atmosphere.

The players were thinking in terms of a figure closer to 10 per cent but in the end they accepted 27 per cent and the resolute Birch had his agreement.

It had been understood that David Batty was one of the main agitators, his agent Hayden Evans claiming that he was devastated by the whole affair. There were further ructions when Eddie Gray said that the former England midfielder did not feature in his first-team plans. When the club tried to negotiate a settlement for the remaining five months of his contract, Batty rejected the proposal out of hand.

There was a dim light at the end of the tunnel: McKenzie announced that Birch had agreed a formal standstill agreement with the club's major creditors until 19 January. It promised enough working capital to tide the club over while it chased new investment. HSBC, the club's bankers, provided a new term loan facility.

Leighton and McKenzie resigned from the board to avoid any conflict of interest – Leighton was interested in a takeover in his own right and there were rumours that McKenzie was seeking funding in South East Asia. Birch confirmed that the club had received an approach from a company associated with Al-Khalifa, which 'may or may not lead to an offer being made for the business'. The Sheikh's group included two Saudi Arabian businessmen and an Asiatic company.

The ambitions of the three men came to nothing, but Birch managed to agree a week's extension to the standstill agreement. He also confirmed that the agreement could be extended by a further fortnight, should the club achieve certain financial goals.

Birch somehow managed to eke the standstill out, week by week, to 27 February with rumours that other potential bidders for the club were circling. It was a tribute to Birch's reputation, abilities and persistence.

Club for Sale

There were claims that Ugandan tycoon Michael Ezra came close to a purchase, even going so far as meetings in the boardroom, before being rejected, but in the end things came down to two Yorkshire-based consortia.

Noises were positive about one of them, headed by former Huddersfield chairman Terry Fisher, known to be a Leeds fan, and supported by former United captain Trevor Cherry. The group curried favour with the fans but three weeks of hints and suggestions ended without a formal offer, believed to be due to a lack of serious funds.

That left the way clear for the other consortium, headed by Leeds-based insolvency practitioner Gerald Krasner. The consortium, known as Adulant Force Limited, completed the purchase of the club on 19 March.

Krasner was appointed chairman of a six-man board which included Leeds legend Peter Lorimer, appointed as a sop to the fans. The other board members were property developers Simon Morris and Melvyn Helme, entrepreneur Melvyn Levi and David Richmond, son of former Bradford chairman Geoffrey, who acted as an unpaid advisor to the consortium. Describing Krasner as 'very straightforward' and 'a tough cookie', Geoffrey Richmond stressed that he would not be joining the new board and was making no investment. It was rumoured, however, that he aspired to the position of chief executive.

Reacting to rumours that Elland Road and Thorp Arch would be sold, Krasner sought to 'categorically' assure fans that United would not be moving from Elland Road. He admitted that contracts were already in place to sell a tract of land at Thorp Arch which wasn't currently used, but there were no further plans to sell the site or move the Academy.

Adulant Force took control of a club deep in relegation trouble. Eddie Gray's appointment in November had brought a new manager bounce and an unbeaten run of five games, but then six straight defeats saw Leeds entrenched at the bottom of the table on 7 February, six points from safety.

A 4-1 defeat of relegation rivals Wolves was a glorious aberration, allowing Leeds to trade positions with the Midlanders as they revived memories of their glory days. Spirited draws with Manchester United and Liverpool hinted that the revival might continue, but a 2-0 defeat at Fulham on 13 March stopped them in their tracks.

The home match on 22 March with Manchester City, eight points above Leeds, was vital, the first game since the takeover.

Gray conjured a passionate performance and a 2-1 victory courtesy of a controversial penalty fifteen minutes from time. Alan Smith clashed with City defender Daniel van Buyten and referee Alan Wiley awarded a penalty despite the contact appearing to be made outside the box. Mark Viduka netted from the penalty spot to lift Leeds off the bottom of the table and within a couple of points of Leicester and Portsmouth.

Could United yet spring another great escape?

A 4-1 defeat at Birmingham suggested not but then Leeds pulled off a breathtaking 3-2 victory against Leicester to draw level with them. When victory at Blackburn saw them go level on points with their opponents and Portsmouth, Leeds appeared to have turned the corner.

Leeds old boy Nigel Martyn returned to Elland Road to inspire a gritty Everton display, pulling out all the stops to help his new club secure a 1-1 draw. It was an opportunity lost and with Portsmouth and Blackburn both winning and Manchester City getting a point at Tottenham, Leeds were a couple of points behind the three with five games remaining.

Leicester and Wolves were cast adrift below United and doomed to relegation, but Gray's men still had a fighting chance.

All their vulnerabilities were laid bare in a 5-0 mauling at unbeaten Arsenal. It was a mortal wound with Leeds fast running out of games. Blackburn and Portsmouth both won the following day and even Manchester City's defeat at home to Southampton was little consolation – the Sky Blues had two points' advantage on Leeds and a goal difference superiority of thirty-one.

The Elland Road game with Portsmouth on 27 April could yet see the Fratton Park club dragged back into the mire (they were five points clear of Leeds) but United took the field more in hope than expectation. Manchester City's failure to win at Leicester the previous day offered hope but Blackburn had virtually guaranteed their safety with victory at Everton.

Safety looked light years away after ten minutes when Yakubu gave Pompey the lead. Leeds were without Viduka, suspended after a dismissal against Leicester, and rookie Simon Johnson was a limited deputy. Smith led the line admirably, but Leeds were poor.

Yakubu's goal had come from a free header at the back post which epitomised United's frailties, and the visitors extended their lead five minutes after half-time, encouraged by more nervy defending. After failing to clear a corner, the Leeds players stood frozen inside their area as Lomana LuaLua followed up a header from Yakubu to force the ball into the net. Elland Road resembled a morgue, deathly quiet and full of pale faces.

In a frantic finish, Ian Harte tucked away an eighty-second-minute penalty as United fought for their lives, but it was all to no avail. The 2-1 defeat left Leeds needing a miracle. When Manchester City beat Newcastle on 1 May they were six points clear. The Whites had three games left to City's two, but their massively superior goal difference added another point to the equation.

The trip to Bolton the following day was suddenly last chance saloon.

There was some encouragement with the return of Viduka and the Aussie opened the scoring with a twenty-seventh-minute penalty after Emerson Thome felled Smith inside Bolton's box. The optimism was short-lived, the odds turning massively against Leeds six minutes later, when Viduka picked up the season's least forgivable red card.

After a booking for kicking out at Thome, Viduka lost the plot completely, ignoring teammates' pleas to calm down. He tripped Ivan Campo and then raised his arm to Bruno N'Gotty. There was a whiff of manic self-destruction in the air, as if he was willing the referee to end his season for him.

All over the place in defence even before Viduka's dismissal, Leeds were in tatters thereafter. The eight minutes following the restart were a nightmare as they surrendered three goals in quick succession.

French import Youri Djorkaeff started the decline after two minutes and added his second almost immediately. When Harte conceded an own goal, the game was up. A fourth goal courtesy of Kevin Nolan with twelve minutes of the game left was not needed but told everybody that Leeds' top-flight era was done.

A hurry scurry 3-3 draw with Charlton formalised Leeds' demotion. Alan Smith had left the Reebok Stadium weeping inconsolably but he was feted as a hero against the Addicks. Captain for the day and scorer of United's third goal, Smith was mobbed by hundreds of fans who broke through the security cordon and onto the pitch to bid a fond farewell to a player they had taken to their hearts.

It was twenty minutes before Smith finally made it back to the sanctuary of the tunnel, prompting Gray to comment, 'Alan's a local hero, a local boy, and you expect that. He will be disappointed we never won the match ... He has been here since he was a kid and everybody knows he believes in the football club. He has been a smashing player and a good lad for Leeds United. His teammates and the fans will be sorry to see him go.'

A fourteen-year stay in the top flight was over. 'Going down but we'll be back,' they sang, but few believed it. Three years after appearing in the last four of the Champions League, Leeds United contemplated life in the second tier with a genuine anxiety that their fall had yet to bottom out.

CHAPTER SIX
Just Me and Gary Kelly

The Adulant Force takeover fooled nobody. It might have allowed the crippling debt to be slashed from an eye-watering £115 million to £20 million, but Leeds were still struggling to pay their way and faced an uncertain future. And there was little togetherness between the members of the consortium – theirs was not a marriage made in heaven.

David Richmond, the biggest single shareholder with 32 per cent, admitted they did not have sufficient resources to buy the club. They hadn't done their homework sufficiently and had gambled too much on a twenty-year season ticket scheme which turned out to be a dismal failure.

Gerling agreed to take a settlement of 10p in the pound on the £21.3 million it was owed and the bondholders settled for £12.6 million up front and a set of conditional future payments to settle their £60 million loan. HMRC would be paid by instalment along with other minor debtors including former managers. All the club's former shareholders, including Professor John McKenzie, saw their 'assets' wiped out at a stroke.

The men forming the consortium put up £4.8 million of their own money to provide working capital, with further personal guarantees of £5 million. They borrowed another £15 million from former Watford chairman Jack Petchey, secured against the Elland Road stadium.

It was clear long before relegation was confirmed that there would be a fire sale of players in the summer, primarily to rid the club of their sky-high salaries. Relegation merely deepened the degree of the cuts. Richmond revealed that there were sixty professionals at Leeds, fifteen of them paid £1 million or more. Such extravagance was unsustainable, especially now in a division where payrolls below £5 million were not uncommon.

David Richmond ruled out any suggestion that the consortium might try to renegotiate contracts, although the likes of Batty, Bridges and Wilcox would not be offered new deals when they expired in the summer, saving about £11 million a year.

The board announced that it had hired agent Phillip Morrison to negotiate player departures on its behalf until 16 May, the day after the Premiership season ended.

Alan Smith strongly criticised the move, adamant that no one but he would decide which club he joined should he make the decision to leave.

Leeds appointed Morrison to ensure that unscrupulous agents did not profit from any deals as Bernie Mandic had done with Harry Kewell in 2003.

First man out of the door was Paul Robinson, off to Spurs for £2 million, followed quickly by Smith, moving to bitter rivals Manchester United in exchange for £7 million. That horrified the Leeds supporters, who vented their rage that all Smith's kissing of the badge had been nothing but a sham.

The departures continued: Mark Viduka to Middlesbrough, James Milner to Newcastle, Stephen McPhail to Barnsley, Ian Harte to Levante in Spain, Nick Barmby to Hull, Dominic Matteo to Blackburn, Danny Mills to Manchester City.

Middlesbrough insisted that England international Michael Ricketts was included as makeweight in the Viduka deal. In his two years with Leeds, Ricketts managed just two League Cup goals.

Although the entire team that played in the Champions League semi-finals was gone, the club was still paying the price for former follies. To secure the deals, Leeds agreed to subsidise some of the salaries, emphasising the desperation of their position. It cost £1.7 million to convince Barmby, who had two years remaining on a lucrative contract, to leave, while Mills' impending move to Manchester City would cost Leeds £2 million over five years.

Kevin Blackwell began his rebuilding plans even before his substantive appointment as manager. He had been keeping the seat warm ever since the departure of Eddie Gray on 10 May. Confirmation of Blackwell's appointment was delayed by uncertainty over exactly who he would be working for.

The media were briefed that Blackwell would be available to discuss his new role on 26 May, but there was a sudden about face.

A meeting with Simon Morris quashed hopes of a quick appointment and left Blackwell in limbo. Morris, who owned 53 per cent of the club with Melvyn Levi, was understood to be unhappy with the speed with which Leeds had planned to announce a successor to Gray.

It was not the first time that Morris and Levi had flexed their muscles. They were behind the departure of Geoffrey Richmond, cast aside at the end of April. It was clear that his aspirations for a major role at the club were seen by Morris and Levi as a power grab.

The issue caused a rift with son David and on 12 July he resigned in order to 'get my life back'. He quit after the gates to his home were padlocked by disenchanted supporters as part of a campaign aimed at driving him away from Elland Road. Richmond described it as 'the worst year of my life,' saying it had affected his health and his family. If he could have his time again, he would not have got involved. He claimed he was owed 'an awful lot of money, running into many hundreds of thousands of pounds'.

His departure caused little heartache, with many remembering him as the man who said that James Milner, 'the face of Leeds United', was not for sale 'at any price' shortly before he was sold to Newcastle.

Krasner said, 'He has done a wonderful job with the players and without him, we would have big, big problems.'

Levi and Morris cast doubt on Blackwell's appointment, despite his being interviewed and enjoying the support of Krasner and Richmond.

Krasner had been clear from his arrival that he was prepared to listen to offers from investors and there were almost immediate discussions with Steve Parkin, owner of Brighouse-based Clipper Logistics. Parkin wanted a controlling interest and it was rumoured that a deal was agreed in principle on 19 May but the board changed their minds and decided to soldier on, viewing Parkin's £20 million offer as too low.

Parkin criticised Krasner for breaking a confidentiality agreement, but the deal was briefly resurrected with the money upped to £25 million.

Parkin revealed later how close he came to taking over and went as far as interviewing then Crystal Palace boss Iain Dowie for the manager's job. He said the deal fell through after his consortium discovered the cost of taking control of the debt-ridden club could have been as high as £50 million.

'I had so many discussions with everyone else, from Geoffrey Richmond to his son, Simon Morris and Melvin Helme, but never with Krasner. I put together a consortium and we had a fair amount of wealth within that to do a deal. We were willing to take it on and be the guarantor for the debt, but we needed to look at the books. They weren't releasing the information to us. What they were saying was show us your funds and we'll show you the books. But I was saying if you don't show me the books, how do I know how much money I need.

'Every day they were coming back and asking for different things, lifetime memberships of the club, directors' seats for life ... When we started the process of doing the refinancing, we committed £5 million of our own money between us, five of us, so that was £1 million each.

'The whole content of the remortgage was based on the ground and Thorp Arch being worth a set amount of money. But there was no way we would ever be able to refinance on the basis of the figures that were brandished about. From where we thought it was at with the refinancing and what the actual figure was, there was a big gap.

'How close were we? I would say we were within days of signing to take over the club. We had already discussed infrastructures. It is common knowledge now that a certain manager – Iain Dowie – was offered the job. That's true, I offered him the job.'

As soon as it was clear that Parkin's deal was dead in the water, the club confirmed the appointment of Blackwell, though he would only sign the contract after speaking to those who had harboured doubts about him. He received a personal apology from Morris.

'In July the club was just me and Gary Kelly' was a quote regularly attributed to Blackwell. It wasn't entirely true, but while Michael Duberry, Lucas Radebe, Eirik Bakke and Seth Johnson (the latter two both injured) were also still on the payroll, pulling together a squad able to compete in the Championship was an unenviable job. Blackwell spoke of not settling for second best, but he couldn't fill the bench for the first game until he signed Brian Deane, Craig Hignett and Steve Guppy at 12.30 p.m. the day before. At one point, his first-team squad included four players on £500 a week.

There were unproven youngsters like Frazer Richardson, Aaron Lennon, Matthew Kilgallon, Simon Johnson, Scott Carson and Jamie McMaster but Blackwell had to scratch around football's bargain bins to pad out a makeshift squad. Most of the sixty-four trialists were swiftly discarded with Blackwell insisting that only 'special players can make it at Elland Road'. Others who passed his test included Neil Sullivan, Stephen Crainey, Clarke Carlisle, Paul Butler, Sean Gregan, Jermaine Wright, Julian Joachim, Danny Pugh and Matthew Spring.

There were precious few names there to excite the emotions, but somehow Leeds won their opening game against Derby with a goal in the last quarter from Richardson as Blackwell handed out seven debuts.

Such a ragbag assortment of players couldn't sustain a meaningful promotion push and there were only three more victories in the first sixteen games. By the beginning of November, Leeds were eighteenth in the table, four points above the relegation places.

Blackwell finally managed to sign his main target, Preston striker David Healy, a Northern Ireland international. The final fee was £650,000 with Preston hard-balling the offers up from an initial £100,000. He brought a sharpness to the front line.

Sunderland midfielder John Oster came in on loan and he and Healy inspired an impressive 4-2 victory at Preston North End on 6 November with Healy netting twice against his former club. The pair also shone when Leeds beat QPR 6-1 on 20 November, but the star of the show was thirty-six-year-old

Deane, whose four-goal salvo had the Elland Road faithful singing his praises. Finally, Blackwell had a team playing the way he wanted.

Oster's stay at Leeds was abruptly terminated for disciplinary reasons. He was released with a police caution following his arrest during a drunken brawl outside a nightclub and he was then called to task after incidents at the club's Christmas party.

Oster's misfortune created an unexpected opportunity for young winger Aaron Lennon.

Turning professional with Leeds in July 2003, Lennon became the youngest player ever to appear in the Premier League when he made his debut as a substitute against Tottenham Hotspur two months later. He went on to make twenty-seven Championship appearances.

Leeds, while remaining in the bottom eight and looking nervously over their shoulders, appeared to have turned a corner though money problems continued to dog the club.

In October, the board negotiated a twenty-five-year sale-and-leaseback deal on Thorp Arch to provide cash headroom. It was sold to an unnamed property investment company with Leeds retaining an option to buy back the land if its financial situation improved. Krasner claimed the deal freed up £4 million.

At the beginning of November, it appeared that the board had finally found a long-term solution to their financial difficulties.

Banker and restaurateur Sebastien Sainsbury launched a takeover, backed by Nova Financial Partners, a US-based organisation. Sainsbury was expected to give Steve Parkin a board role if his bid succeeded.

Parkin would join Nova president Michael Lucas and Sainsbury as three of nine executives on a new board. Three non-executive roles would be created, including one reserved for a Leeds United supporter, to be determined by ballot.

Negotiations were complicated by the imminent payment of £2.5 million to Jack Petchey. His loan was secured on Elland Road via a debenture mortgage with Trefick Ltd, his investment vehicle. Trefick loaned £15 million to help fund the takeover, the terms demanding a hefty £1.5 million a month in interest.

There were positive noises about Sainsbury's bid, but there was friction between him and some of United's directors.

Sainsbury warned the board that if they did not accept his deal they would be forced to sell Elland Road. They should make a decision in the best interests of the shareholders, the players and particularly the fans, he insisted.

Krasner confirmed that discussions were continuing with various parties, but nothing had been signed. The board insisted that any interested party must be able to confirm that the necessary funds were available to complete any transaction. 'Despite much press speculation, as we stand now, no party has met our conditions.'

Morris admitted that the club had received a letter from a lawyer in Ontario, though he had not yet been formally engaged. He was representing a third-party broker from Florida who had been instructed by Nova. The lawyer said that he understood $50 million was available but he could not confirm this himself.

Morris scoffed at the letter, insisting that the board had yet to receive proof of funds. It was important for people to understand that the club had squandered hundreds of thousands on previous bids without seeing proof of funds and were not prepared to do so again. The board were content to sit down with any party that could prove they had the necessary backing.

Sainsbury hit back on BBC Radio Five Live, saying, 'We made a formal offer to buy Leeds and agreed terms and conditions and it would appear today the conditions have changed. They said [it was because] of proof of funds but they were offered a £500,000 non-refundable deposit on Wednesday. If that money didn't arrive, they could tear up any agreement we had.'

Shortly before kick-off of Leeds' game at Preston in November, Radio Aire carried an exclusive interview with Sainsbury, who insisted a deal had been agreed by United and Nova. A contract would be signed two days later and the deal completed by the transfer of funds on Thursday. Sainsbury claimed the agreement was reached at 2.00 p.m. in the boardroom at Deepdale, Preston North End's stadium.

After the game there was an acrimonious falling out on air between Sainsbury and Melvyn Helme, the two men interrupting each other and openly bickering.

Helme said, 'We can't sign any contract until we've seen proof of funds, Mr Sainsbury is well aware of that.'

Sainsbury responded, 'That is not what you have just agreed with Mr Lucas in front of other people … We will transfer the funds on completion on Thursday.'

Helme scoffed, 'Mike Lucas told me we were completing on Monday and now it's Thursday,' and the argument continued.

A joint statement confirmed that Nova had agreed to transfer £25 million into their solicitors' bank account by the end of Thursday. The deal was set to complete by 1.00 p.m. on Friday 12 November, in time to repay Petchey.

There were clearly issues between the two parties and the emergence of a rival consortium, headed by local builder Norman Stubbs, only exacerbated the friction.

Stubbs' deal was based on the sale of Elland Road – he had raised £10 million and the proposed sale and leaseback of the stadium was expected to bring in a further £15 million. However, Stubbs' backers insisted all monies must be directed towards the continued survival of the club rather than rewarding the existing directors.

Krasner was happy with Stubbs' offer, but his view was not shared by two of the others who pushed exclusively for Sainsbury's consortium, which offered two seats on the board and a £2 million sweetener.

With financial analysts forecasting that the club would fall into administration by March unless £13 million outstanding to Petchey and £9 million owed to HMRC was cleared, the future looked as unclear as ever for Leeds United.

CHAPTER SEVEN
Ken Bates

12 November 2004: Gerald Krasner has just announced that his board has sold the Elland Road stadium to raise the cash to keep Leeds United Football Club trading.

The board had expected to complete the sale of the club to Sebastien Sainsbury at 1.00 p.m. but when it failed to do so, the directors had little alternative other than to use the stadium as collateral to raise the funds to enable them to clear a £9.2 million debt owed to Jack Petchey.

Krasner defended both the board's record and its latest decision. The sale allowed them to reduce the club's debt to less than £25 million from a starting point of £104 million when the consortium took over. Without his board there would have been no Leeds United, said Krasner. They had kept the club afloat and were stabilising the position. When they arrived, he claimed, there had been no money to pay the players and they had to find the cash to clear the arrears. If they had not come up with the wages, the players would have been entitled to walk away and Leeds would have collapsed.

Krasner insisted that 'football remains at Elland Road. We have ensured that we have the option to not only use the ground in the long term, but to purchase back the ground when the opportunity arises.'

Norman Stubbs left for a holiday on 13 November confident that his pursuit of Leeds United would be successful.

But the club was still struggling to pay its way, with £1.2 million payable to the HMRC by 15 December and a further £800,000 required to settle a VAT bill. To buy time, Kevin Blackwell agreed to sell promising young keeper Scott Carson to Liverpool.

On 10 January, a new actor entered the fray. *The Independent* reported that former Chelsea owner Ken Bates wanted to make one final foray into big-time football by buying a majority share in Leeds.

When he stepped down as Chelsea chairman the previous March, it left a vacuum in his life after almost forty years in the game. An attempt to take control of Sheffield Wednesday had come to nothing and Bates was eager to find a new quarry. He had discussed involvement in Sebastien Sainsbury's consortium.

Bates had been in the Italian bar of the Dorchester Hotel in London having a drink with Ashraf Marwan, a former Chelsea shareholder, when John Owen, an old friend, walked in and told him that Sainsbury wanted to meet him.

Bates agreed to a meeting in which Sainsbury revealed his plans. He asked Bates whether he was interested in a piece of the action. Bates, still flush from the sale of Chelsea, said he had £10 million available but would only get involved if he could purchase a controlling interest. No surprise there; one famous quote about Bates claimed that he believed in a committee of two – with one absent. When Bates asked who the other members of the consortium were, Sainsbury refused to reveal their identities. Bates said he wasn't giving £10 million to people he didn't know and that was that.

Three days later, Sainsbury issued a statement saying that he had ended his interest in Leeds United, claiming that due diligence identified previously unknown liabilities of £10 million. His exit cleared the way for Stubbs' consortium.

Krasner was scathing about Sainsbury and Nova. 'We asked them to put up £50,000 towards our costs by 5.00 p.m. on Thursday and at 4.45 p.m., they pulled out. They could not find the £50,000 even. They were running a media campaign despite confidentiality agreements with us. It was impossible to seriously negotiate with them.'

On 18 January, it was reported that the club had ten days to avoid administration, with its future dependent on Stubbs stalling the demands of the tax authorities and other creditors.

Stubbs held fresh talks with the board and proposed investing around £10 million including £5 million from Allan Leighton. Things were dragging, prompting some to suggest that Leighton was waiting until the club went into administration before launching a cut-price move.

Suddenly Bates emerged as the man in the box seat. He opened discussions with Krasner and the other directors as soon as Sainsbury dropped out of the running.

On 17 January, Krasner and Melvyn Levi met Bates at the London offices of Bates' lawyer, Mark Taylor. Two days later Bates set off for Yorkshire in what he described as 'a cloak and dagger operation ... We get off the train at Wakefield, get into this BMW and are driven into the underground car park at the Leeds lawyer's office. Then through the trade entrance and into the office where we have a meeting for nine hours. Then we are driven to a hotel

... The Leeds lawyer checks me in, the room being booked in his name and nobody has seen me enter the hotel.

'Trevor Birch comes up to my suite to have dinner. I go into the bedroom. Yvonne [Todd, his finance director at Chelsea] has come up, she orders the food and I stay in the bedroom and talk to Trevor. Next morning this guy picks up my bags, pays and we head for the cars and back to the lawyer's office without anyone noticing I was in the hotel.'

Krasner was so confident that the Bates deal would go ahead that he started drafting a press release. What clinched things was a guarantee from Bates that the £4.5 million owed in directors' loans would be quickly repaid, although that came to nothing.

In the early hours of Friday 21 January, Bates completed his takeover, paying £4.9 million for 50 per cent of the shares. The terms of the agreement with the bondholders were such that if there had been a full buyout, they would have been entitled to a significant penalty payment. Bates agreed to bide his time, with the balance of the shares to be transferred in May when the conditions expired.

Bates insisted that he was not putting in any money himself, but merely fronting the purchase for an anonymous Geneva-based organisation, Forward Sports Fund. Most informed critics viewed Forward as one of Bates' opaque shell companies, similar to those he had employed during his time with Chelsea. No one really understood Bates' stubborn obsession with such labyrinthine schemes, but it was doubtless a means of garnering some sort of financial advantage.

'I wouldn't like us to get promoted this season,' said Bates after completing the transaction. 'If you go up too soon, you only come down again. Maybe if we can win promotion in the next couple of seasons, establish ourselves in the Premiership, get a top six place and go back into Europe.'

Bates said he intended to run the club from his home in Monte Carlo and would only attend home matches. 'I've done a deal with a lovely local jet plane service. Leave here at 8.00 a.m. on Wednesday, get to Bradford-Leeds airport by 9.30. I will be at Leeds at 10, work Wednesday, Thursday, Friday and Saturday and get the plane back at 7 o'clock, 11 o'clock back here in time for last orders at the pub, crash out on Sunday. I will be in Leeds for four days but have spent only two days in the country.' As a tax exile, Bates could spend only ninety full days per year in the UK.

'Having worked with Ken, he will give it his total attention,' Trevor Birch told *The Yorkshire Post*. 'He hates to fail; he will have one objective in mind which is to return the club to the Premier League, and knowing him, he will want to redevelop the stadium. Stamford Bridge is testament to that ... In 2005, Leeds being the city it is should have a football team with a football ground that is state of the art and defines the city. It seems to me a lost opportunity. When you come up on the train from London and look across, it is an eyesore. How good would a redeveloped stadium have been for the city?'

Birch thought Bates stood to gain little from his involvement other than personal satisfaction. 'At seventy-three, Ken has not done this as a means of getting rich. It's all about him having one last project, which will be to return Leeds to its rightful position ultimately.'

News of Bates' involvement was anathema to many supporters. After United fans damaged a scoreboard at Stamford Bridge in 1984, Bates promised, 'I shall not rest until Leeds United are kicked out of the Football League. Their fans are the scum of the Earth, absolute animals and a disgrace. I will do everything in my power to make this happen.'

There were also concerns about his chequered past, some dubious business dealings and the aggressive way he dealt with friends and foes alike.

The press conference held following the takeover was typical Bates, with the new owner in bombastic mood. There were snide put-downs of press representatives, some smart one-liners and an insistence that Leeds would closely guard its financial plans. He promised the fans a 'lorra lorra laughs' and claimed that he and Kevin Blackwell had exchanged home and mobile telephone numbers 'as lovers do … The footballing decisions are his.'

Bates had moved on from an earlier declaration that former goalkeepers don't make good managers – as a custodian himself, Blackwell feared the worst when he heard that one.

Despite considerable opposition, no one could doubt that Bates' intervention saved Leeds from financial ruin. When he arrived, the team were fourteenth in the table and the ten-point penalty that administration would have brought would have dumped them in the bottom three. His first game brought victory courtesy of a single goal at Stoke.

Bates funded Blackwell to bring in reinforcements with Blackburn's former England left-back Michael Gray, West Brom striker Rob Hulse and Marlon King of Forest all arriving on loan. Combative Crystal Palace midfielder Shaun Derry had come in before Christmas, and Leeds looked a much better side, with Hulse scoring twice on his debut in a 3-1 defeat of promotion-chasing Reading.

The Stoke result saw Leeds up to an unlikely tenth, four points off the play-offs, but they fell away with a single win in the final ten games and ended the season fourteenth.

That was the side's true level at that time. The season brought twenty-eight debuts and sixty-four trialists, according to Blackwell, 'including a Dutch winger who lasted ten minutes at Macclesfield because I realised he must have been a waiter, and to go through all that was just incredible. I kept thinking, "This cannot be right." We've got state-of-the-art facilities at Leeds and yet we cannot get any players in.'

Giving weight to his reputation as a skinflint, Bates declared that Leeds would not select Seth Johnson again as to do so would trigger a £250,000 payment to Derby under the terms of his transfer.

Said Blackwell, 'It is nearly four years that Seth has been here and he's only made fifty-nine appearances in that time through no fault of his own because he's been plagued by injuries. To spend £250,000 on a player for the next three games who will not affect our season one way or another ... would not be prudent. I was desperate for him to play in the last three games and we rang Derby to see if they would extend the payment trigger to sixty-three games but they wouldn't.'

On a more positive note, Bates proclaimed himself satisfied with progress. 'We had a scrap team – youngsters, free signings and players on loan – all put together by Kevin Blackwell and they have been fantastic. At half-time on Boxing Day, we were actually in the relegation zone and since that time we have scored enough points to be in the play-offs. That augurs well for next season.

'I have great confidence in Kevin Blackwell, he took over as manager and had very little to play with and the job he has done this season has been outstanding. He deserves the opportunity to start next season with a level playing field. Kevin Blackwell has my unqualified support; I told the players that on the first home game since I took over and that remains unchanged.'

CHAPTER EIGHT
Dead Cat Bounce

'We have been linked with a lot of big players in the last week or so and I can't dispute that we are interested in the players.'

Kevin Blackwell, responding to questions about what the summer of 2005 might bring, acknowledged that the club's name would be used by unscrupulous agents to influence the market and get the best deal for their clients. His need to improve a mid-table squad made rumours an inevitability.

Ken Bates was happy to devote the final year's parachute payment to Blackwell's transfer ambitions and Rob Hulse's loan deal was made permanent as the first step. Blackwell added Eddie Lewis, Steve Stone, Jonathan Douglas, Ian Moore, Dan Harding, Rui Marques, Richard Cresswell, Robbie Blake and Ian Bennett. It gave the squad a fresh, go-ahead look.

Leeds got off to a decent start with seven wins from the first thirteen games and looked good in doing so. Stone and Cresswell suffered injuries and Harding a crisis of confidence, but Lewis, Douglas and Blake looked good buys. Leeds were third by mid-October, seven points off the automatic promotion spots.

A real test of their promotion credentials came when Leeds hosted table-topping Sheffield United, managed by Blackwell's former boss, Neil Warnock. The pair had fallen out after Blackwell's defection to Elland Road in 2003 and Warnock claimed that Leeds had nipped in to scupper his attempt to buy Cresswell as part of some personal feud.

Blackwell laughed the accusations off as immature mind games with honours shared in a thundering 1-1 draw. A point apiece was a fair reflection of play, though Leeds were disappointed not to have three after giving one of their best performances of the season.

'I said before the game that this was a benchmark as to how the club has moved forward,' smiled Blackwell. 'Sheffield United have been building for a long time but inside nine months we are competing at the top end of the division. It was a cracking game, like the old days in the Premiership. We knew it would be tough but we more than competed and could easily have won. We scored a great goal but there was some poor defending for theirs. We're better than that and it's frustrating.'

In the five games that followed, Leeds managed just two goals and three points. A tame goalless draw at home to Preston on Bonfire Night left Leeds sixth. The only positive note came with a promising debut by Irish international midfielder Liam Miller.

Blackwell had seen red after a poor performance ended in defeat at second bottom Crewe on 1 November. 'I have let the players know that I can't tolerate that,' he snapped. 'If they think they can play sixteen or seventeen good games and then have one day off they are wrong ... There's no one going to rest on their laurels at this football club thinking they've got the shirt and that's it because I've only got nineteen players. That's not good enough for me and it won't be good enough for them.'

Days later, the club announced the loan signing of twenty-four-year-old Miller from Manchester United, where he had been declared surplus to requirements by Sir Alex Ferguson.

Miller had some good moments against Preston and showed the creativity that United had been lacking. There was a two-week international break after the match and Blackwell took his men away for a friendly in France to freshen things up. They beat Rodez 1-0 and Miller impressed the manager again. 'He's box to box, he likes a tackle and if he gets into the last third unnoticed it'll be interesting to see how he does. I knew he wasn't playing regularly at Manchester United and it's about getting as many games as he can while he is here.'

United's return to action brought a tough-looking trip to relegated Southampton. While the Saints had drawn too many games as they chased an instant return to the Premiership, they had only suffered two defeats and were dangerous opponents.

A 30,000-plus crowd anticipated a victory for the home team and after twenty-seven minutes, Southampton earned the breakthrough their promising football deserved.

The pace of teenage starlet Theo Walcott unsettled the United defence and his low cross had to be hacked behind by a back-pedalling Gary Kelly. From Quashie's looping corner, Svensson looked to have misfired badly with his header back across goal, but an unmarked Pahars headed in from an acute angle.

Within eight minutes, the Saints added a second and again Walcott's pace was key. He was released down the right by Quashie and raced past Kilgallon. He pulled the ball across goal for the unmarked Quashie to sidefoot round a rooted Neil Sullivan from 15 yards.

Things worsened on the stroke of half-time. The fourth official had just signalled two minutes' added time when a cruelly exposed Dan Harding moved to block Matt Oakley's header with his arms raised. Inevitably, the referee awarded a penalty.

Quashie wasn't fazed by Neil Sullivan's antics in goal and blasted the ball high into the right-hand corner of the net.

Leeds were 3-0 down and rocking. Only a miracle could save them now …

After the resumption, a fourth from Southampton looked more likely than any United revival with Sullivan having to save at point blank from Brett Ormerod.

The match seemed certain to peter out into a boring formality with twenty minutes or so remaining but United found a reviving spark. In the sixty-seventh minute Miller blazed a free kick from the edge of the area narrowly over the Southampton bar. Blackwell had already decided to make a change and threw Healy on for Richardson, opting to play him in a three up top with Hulse and Blake.

The Irishman prompted some stirrings of life and won a corner as the clock ticked on to seventy-one minutes. Kelly's high cross was met perfectly by Butler in the middle, 8 yards out, and his header looped over a Saints defender and into the net.

Though optimistic United fans chanted gleefully, 'We're going to win 4-3,' it looked like the goal would be mere consolation. However, it brought divine inspiration – confidence came flooding back as the Saints started to wobble.

With thirteen minutes left, United snatched a second. A deep ball from the left was not dealt with and dropped to Healy on the right corner of the area. His angled shot across the penalty box fell perfectly for Blake to turn home his third goal of the season.

The Saints were now all over the place and incredibly, after eighty-four minutes, Leeds were level. Healy was again at the heart of a move deep inside the danger zone and fired against Danny Higginbotham's hand. The referee had no hesitation in pointing to the spot and Healy fired the penalty into the roof of the net.

There was only one side in it now – the Saints were a shambles.

With four minutes to go, and only fifteen since they had been 3-0 down, Leeds snatched a fourth goal. Hulse pulled the ball back across the area from the right and a deflection took it to Miller 12 yards out. He drove it home precisely, leaving goalkeeper Niemi completely flat-footed.

That was the signal for celebrations as players, staff and fans joined together in ecstatic frenzy to mark the comeback of the season.

Leeds secured the most memorable of victories without a scare. Kevin Blackwell was over the moon at the end, saying, 'It's up there with the top victories I've been involved in.'

Building on the result, Leeds won eight times in the next eleven to consolidate third spot, which they held from 28 December to 4 February. They were eleven points behind second-placed Sheffield United but thirteen ahead of Cardiff in seventh, odds-on for a place in the play-offs.

Chances of automatic promotion were scuppered by a stuttering run which yielded a single victory from the final ten games, derailed by a lack of goals. Nevertheless, the team had enough points in the bag and a goalless draw at home to Plymouth on 8 April guaranteed a play-off place.

Bates rewarded Blackwell with a three-year contract. Prompted by rumours of interest from Leicester and Derby, Bates agreed the deal during a meeting in Monaco on 7 March.

'I'm a big believer that if it ain't broke you don't mend it,' said Bates. 'Kevin wasn't going to be allowed to go anywhere else.'

Blackwell pronounced himself 'delighted. I feel the club is only at the start of something good. I'm positive that we can go on and achieve good things … I wouldn't have signed this if it wasn't for Ken Bates. A lot of people were quick to write us off in terms of working together, but I really feel I'm part of the future at Leeds now. I never spoke to the chairman about a new contract. He said he would do something when he felt the time was right and I took him at his word.'

The play-off semi-final paired Leeds with a dogged Preston side. The Deepdale team had secured twenty-six points from their final ten matches and were the division's form team, finishing with the best defensive record. When they defeated Leeds 2-0 in the final match at Deepdale, they leapfrogged United into fourth, securing home advantage for the decisive second leg.

Blackwell had sent out a reserve side in that game, keeping his powder dry for the bigger test to come, but when North End striker David Nugent scored a brilliant individual goal in the Elland Road first leg, it looked like Blackwell's strategies would come to naught. Nugent made the breakthrough in the forty-eighth minute, taking on and beating the entire United defence with his pace and trickery.

Eddie Lewis dug United out of a hole with a wonderfully placed curling free kick with sixteen minutes left. The teams would start on level terms at Deepdale with away goals having no part under the play-off rules.

The reaction of Preston boss Billy Davies and his staff at the end showed how much the result meant. The little Scot said, 'It's a tremendous result for us, we can ask for no more, we've come here, done the job. It now swings towards our favour.'

Blackwell set Leeds out at Deepdale with Rob Hulse spearheading a 4-5-1 formation designed to frustrate. If the Lancastrians thought that the hardest part of the job had been done in Yorkshire, they soon realised they were in for a battle royal on the fifth anniversary of United's Champions League semi-final clash with Valencia.

There was an unlovely tension between the two teams – Gregan, Healy, substitute Cresswell and Lewis were all former Preston men. It was obvious that everyone was fired up for the occasion and there was a spate of running battles. Referee Mike Thorpe seemed content to let the players take the law into their own hands early on and ill feeling boiled over. Gregan and Danny Dichio were at each other's throats throughout, while Nugent and Kilgallon seemed to believe their main responsibility was winding each other up. A challenge by Lewis on Claude Davis left the Preston centre-back requiring treatment and the partisan home crowd baying their rage.

Shaun Derry was the first to see his name go into the referee's book after thirty minutes for a lunge on Marcus Stewart. In the closing minutes of the half, Kilgallon and Nugent joined him after a spiteful kick and push on the edge of the penalty area. A less lenient referee might have gone for a more serious sanction.

As the official blew for half-time, Deepdale and the surrounding streets were plunged into darkness by a substation failure that took twenty-five minutes to resolve. There were worried looks as time dragged by – neither camp wanted an abandonment and the players struggled to stay match sharp in the break.

The teams eventually came back out for the restart at 9.10 with Preston bringing Patrick Agyemang on for Stewart.

The delay had a greater impact on Preston than it did on United, who came out with increased tempo and attacking intent. After Gregan was booked for blocking off Nugent's run in the opening seconds, Leeds shook North End with some concerted attacking, and took the lead after fifty-six minutes.

United won a corner on the right, and as Kelly took it Derry was appealing for a foul after appearing to be obstructed. The Preston defence was distracted and Hulse had an acre of space to run into from the back post and made the most of it. He rose to nod the ball perfectly into the bottom left-hand corner as Nash remained rooted in the centre of the goal.

It was the first Preston concession at Deepdale in 568 minutes and shattered their confidence, allowing Leeds to press home their advantage just after the hour mark.

Miller touched the ball through a defender's legs to Hulse on the left of the area. He burst through a non-existent challenge and held off Mawene to fire the ball low across the 6-yard box. Davis got a touch to the cross but it reached Richardson in space at the far post. He had time to trap and fire goalwards from 6 yards out. Nash reached the shot but its pace took it beneath him to give United a 2-0 advantage.

The score looked decisive, but Preston hopes were raised when Crainey was sent off after sixty-nine minutes for a second bookable offence. He had received his first caution five minutes earlier for dissent – his second came for bringing Nugent down on the way towards the area. Miller was booked for protesting the decision.

When Cresswell came on for a tiring Hulse after seventy-eight minutes, he was harshly booked within a minute.

Preston thought they had pulled one back when Mears headed home an Alexander corner. The goal was disallowed, the referee ruling that the corner had curled out of play before reaching the far post.

It was then down to the far end and an ugly-looking challenge by Cresswell on keeper Nash. The striker had little choice other than to go for the loose ball but left Nash with a broken cheekbone, provoking a mass brawl in the Preston goal area. Strangely, referee Thorpe chose to book Kelly and Douglas, letting Cresswell off scot free. Arguably, Nash and Davis merited a caution for their part in the conflict, and it was bizarre that United now had eight men in the referee's book to one from Preston.

The toll increased further when Cresswell fell foul of the official as the game ticked into injury-time. He tussled with a Preston defender and when the decision went against him he kicked the ball away in an ill-advised attempt to kill time. He protested long and hard but Thorpe was adamant and left United clinging on for six minutes of injury-time with nine men.

The heat had gone out of Preston's efforts and they struggled to manufacture an opportunity. As the final whistle sounded, the United party and their fervent supporters threw their arms skyward, celebrating their place in the Millennium final.

Kevin Blackwell: 'I'm extremely proud. The lads were fantastic. They showed true grit and determination to get through here ... It was a game that had everything. There was a power cut, delays, goals disallowed, tackles, bookings and a referee that seemed to lose his way right at the end. I wasn't sure we would have players left the way he was going on.'

Blackwell revealed the tactics used to gee his men up for the game. After Billy Davies' touchline celebration at Elland Road, Leeds required no greater motivation. Memories of Davies celebrating in front of the Preston fans were etched into the players' minds, and steps were taken to ensure they remained there, a notice reading, 'Billy Davies – Job Done' pinned to their dressing room door at Deepdale.

United supporters flocked to Elland Road in their thousands in search of priceless tickets for the final at the Millennium Stadium. It was widely believed that 40,000 of the 65,000 present were Whites supporters and they certainly made their presence felt, making the stadium an extension of Leeds for the day. It was in stark contrast to the average attendance at Elland Road, which had slumped to little more than 22,000, the lowest figure since 1989, the days of the old Second Division.

Blackwell went for a conservative approach, staying with the 4-5-1 formation that had been so effective at Preston. He was forced into one change, recalling fit again captain Paul Butler for the suspended Crainey and switching Kilgallon to left-back.

It was clear from the first few seconds that United's back four would face a torrid afternoon. Watford, playing to their strengths of power and pace, had laid down a specific and very effective game plan. A hard-running midfield four would back up strongly behind the front two of Marlon King and Darius Henderson – at every dead ball opportunity the ball would be launched deep into the heart of the United penalty area for the Hornets to physically contest. They had a long-throw specialist in Gavin Mahon, and exciting wide man Ashley Young was a free kick expert. It was his dead ball strike that had brought the Hornets a lead in the Championship contest at Elland Road.

Watford manager Aidy Boothroyd had identified the United centre-backs as weak links, with a one-paced Gregan and a half-fit Butler forced to turn and chase at every opportunity. Within two minutes, the reinstated skipper was forced to head desperately over his own bar under a robust challenge from Henderson.

Watford were up close and personal, all over United like a rash. They were committed to making life uncomfortable, content to let Leeds have ball and space deep where they could do no damage but harrying mercilessly whenever they advanced into more threatening territory.

The Hornets' midfield quartet – Mahon, Young, Chambers and Spring – settled far more quickly to their work than their anonymous United counterparts. Only Shaun Derry could find his genuine form. Watford's dominance gave them sound foundations, denying United any bolthole from a defensive battle of attrition as the booming dead ball shells rained down on their area.

Watford's possession told after twenty-five minutes following a series of corners. Beefy American centre-back Jay DeMerit was being man-marked by Hulse, but the striker was left holding his head disconsolately in his hands as DeMerit battered his way towards Young's deep corner. No one took responsibility as the cross dropped invitingly and the defender powered home a fierce header from close range.

Watford continued to dominate, retaining possession and picking up all the loose stuff as United players struggled to keep hold of the ball.

Blackwell changed things round at the interval, bringing Blake on for an out-of-touch Richardson and moving to 4-4-2. The change brought not even an occasional ripple to the calm waters of Watford's half. The Hornets came out as strongly as they had finished the first period and Henderson tested Sullivan with a powerful shot.

They went further ahead, virtually ending the match as a contest after fifty-seven minutes. The referee awarded them a throw on the left that should probably have gone to United, and Mahon launched another long ball towards goal.

There was a tangle in the middle and from 8 yards Chambers turned and put in a low shot that ballooned off Lewis and over Sullivan's despairing dive. The ball touched the far post and looked like bouncing out until it ricocheted in off the prostrate keeper's back.

Blackwell brought Healy on for Miller and pushed forward in the vain hope of a revival that was never on the cards. United looked incapable of manufacturing a half-chance, even if the game had lasted double its allotted ninety minutes.

Six minutes from the end, Watford tied things up. Former Leeds loanee Marlon King was released in the area after a quick break and when he cut back across Derry, the midfielder flicked his ankle, sending him to the ground. Derry had enjoyed a spirited afternoon, rallying those about him and at times holding the Hornets at bay on his own. He was the picture of despair as he sat on the turf.

Henderson calmly slotted home the penalty to complete an emphatic 3-0 victory. And that was that ...

United were well beaten on the day, picked apart by a team that was simply more up for it than they. Supporters bitterly berated Kevin Blackwell for his overly cautious approach.

The manager acknowledged their pain, while emphasising the positive improvements made at United. 'It hurts like hell right now. I have been here two times in three years and lost 3-0 both times, but that's not as disappointing as dropping out of the Premiership, seeing everybody leave and nearly losing the club as well. We'll dust ourselves down ... We have put together a side that has proved it can be competitive and we have achieved a lot in the last year. Eighteen months ago, we were among the favourites to go down with Rotherham and Gillingham, but to be in the final here with 40,000 Leeds fans shows how far we have come.'

CHAPTER NINE
The Stuff of Nightmares

'In an ideal world, you always keep your best players and then add to them,' said Kevin Blackwell, following the disappointment of missing out in the play-offs. 'But it isn't an ideal world. My track record here has seen people come in for a lot less than what they have left for. We have doubled our money on Rob Hulse. Matthew Spring and Clarke Carlisle came in for nothing ... Simon Walton did not cost us a penny and he brought in around £1 million. My responsibility is to look after the finances of this club and not just the football. When a situation comes along where I can help the club financially, then I have to do it.'

Making such a fist of their second Championship campaign should have been the springboard for Leeds to go one further in 2006/07. The contracts of former players such as Fowler, Keane, Mills and Duberry had expired, reducing the wage bill from £17 million to less than £10 million, and supporters expected a summer of investment. However, the club's parachute payments were exhausted and Ken Bates' commitment to a profitable business model meant that there had to be cuts. Nevertheless, he found the money to develop the South Stand at Elland Road, much to the annoyance of fans.

Promoted Sheffield United spirited away £2.2 million Hulse and Ian Bennett — Neil Warnock wanted Matthew Kilgallon as well, but Leeds held on to the young defender, at least for the time being. There were other departures and Leeds were unquestionably weakened, notwithstanding the introduction of several new men. Luton captain Kevin Nicholls was the most notable arrival, setting Bates back by £700,000. He was injured in a freak training ground clash with Paul Butler and missed the first month of the season. When he attempted a return at the end of September, Nicholls damaged medial knee ligaments and was ruled out until December.

The Stuff of Nightmares

Blackwell padded out his squad with cut-price journeymen like Seb Carole, Ian Westlake, Hayden Foxe, Geoff Horsfield and Tony Warner. He brought in Millwall captain David Livermore for £250,000, but bizarrely let him go to Hull thirteen days later after the signings of Westlake and Nicholls.

When Bates dropped into Blackwell's pre-season staff meeting, he heard them emphasise the limitations of the squad and warn that a relegation battle was on the cards. An incensed Bates gave them short shrift. He told the media that 'from now on we can't blame previous boards, a lack of money or the fact Kevin had only two players when he took over. That's all gone – it doesn't mean a thing.'

It was evident that Bates was in denial and the prophets of doom were soon found to be absolutely spot on. The defeat at Coventry on 16 September was United's fifth reverse in the opening eight matches and left them second bottom. Going back further, the final ten Championship games of the previous season had yielded a single victory. Leeds were sinking like a stone and just got worse, although Blackwell claimed they were starved of luck. He seethed with rage at the lack of fight, saying, 'When the players look in the mirror [they have to be] satisfied they're giving their all to the shirt, the club, and the fans.'

He was confident that he retained the support of Bates. 'Me and the chairman have talked and he knows what I'm doing and I know what he's doing and we're just getting on with it. We know what the plan for the football club is and that the two of us would have to stick together when things got tough and we'd also have to do things for the football club.

'We've had to rein our ambitions in at times and we've thought big at other times – that's when we got the four players in last season, this season we haven't been able to do that so we've taken a rain check on our ambitions. But there's still a buzz about the place. The players here are as honest as the day is long and came at a time when many players wouldn't have come here. I couldn't even guarantee their wages, but they know how big this club is and know what's expected of them – and recent results have hurt.

'Every manager is gauged on results, and right now I have to say that the results haven't been good enough. I have to accept that. I won't hide from it, and every manager goes through it. I haven't changed my management style in any way, and seven games ago I was a top manager. Seven games later I'm not ... We're all slightly mystified how, with the work that we've done, we haven't won more games.'

Four days later, Bates flew in from Monaco to sack Blackwell. After singing his praises and writing in the matchday programme that the dismissal had been one of the most difficult decisions of his career, Bates accused the manager of gross misconduct for complaining publicly about United's financial problems. Bates argued that he had undermined both him and the club.

He refuted Blackwell's claims that he had not been backed financially, saying that the money spent on players since his takeover in 2005 totalled £7.1 million, with a net expenditure of £2.5 million. He insisted that the manager was allowed to sign 'every player he wanted ... Blackwell says he did a fantastic job with no money but that's bollocks. This summer he bought Westlake, Douglas, Nicholls and Livermore – that's over £2 million spent. It's more than any other club spent, apart from the big boys who had their parachute payments. The only player I refused to buy was Nugent because we couldn't afford him.'

Bates slated Blackwell for being unable to control a 'festering' dressing room, 'people causing trouble, making snide remarks'.

Despite long-running speculation that Bates would bring in former Chelsea player Dennis Wise, the chairman gave assistant manager John Carver the nod initially. His first game brought a promising victory against Birmingham but four defeats on the bounce with fifteen goals conceded spelled the end for Carver.

The Geordie hadn't sought the job, saying, 'I knew that the team we had wasn't going to get us out of trouble. But because I had a contract with the club, I couldn't refuse it – you've got a mortgage to pay. I had to go and meet Ken. He said: "You're getting no more money, but if you get us promoted I'll give you a massive bonus." We were in the bottom three, so that was never going to happen.'

Leeds had lost nine of their thirteen games, matching 1946 and 2003 as their worst ever start to a season. They went on to be relegated on both occasions.

Wise was installed as manager on 25 October, bringing with him his assistant, Gus Poyet. Bates was forced to compensate Swindon Town to the tune of £200,000.

The fans were up in arms, urging whoever would listen to 'Get the Chelsea out of Leeds' and informing Bates that 'You can stick Dennis Wise up your a***.'

Ray Fell, chairman of the Leeds United Supporters' Club, suggested that Wise's often hostile conduct as a Chelsea player counted against him with the fans. His playing career included thirteen red cards and an incident that left Leicester teammate Callum Davidson with a broken jaw. 'There is a history in how Wise behaved in matches against Leeds,' he said. 'Speaking to many fans, it seems that he is the very last choice to be manager. We wanted a figure such as Gary McAllister – somebody who at least had a genuine personal connection with the club.'

Wise was undeterred, saying of the players, 'They're down on confidence and I told them I wanted them to be the Leeds of old who were ...' He hesitated, as if trying to settle on the most appropriate phrase ... 'Well, 'orrible ... I want nastiness and togetherness and I've explained that to them ... They're a very talented bunch here and I said to the players I was bewildered by the side's position. I think they understand what they're getting ... I also need to look at what I've got and whether there are players who wish to be at the football club. I need to know who wants to stay and who wants to leave.'

Wise told the press that he had already taken his first difficult decision, relieving Paul Butler of the captaincy and passing the armband to Kevin Nicholls, a man who, because of injuries, had yet to make any telling impression. 'Nicko's the type that I like,' Wise enthused. 'He's got a bit of bite about him. He's very aggressive, a leader. I played against him a couple of times and he booted me – and it hurt. He's a nice fella; he's what I want.'

Nicholls later rewarded Wise by demanding a move back to Luton, claiming that the transfer to Leeds had been a mistake.

Completing the former Chelsea quartet on the press conference platform was Gwyn Williams, who had survived the entire Bates era. Twenty-seven years at Stamford Bridge saw him fill every job from scout to assisting first-time managers such as Ruud Gullit and Gianluca Vialli.

Williams, who knew where all the skeletons were buried at Stamford Bridge, had accepted Bates' invitation to rebuild the playing side at Elland Road, from apprentices to Bosman-type transfers.

'It is,' he said, 'very much like Chelsea all over again.' One of his first tasks at Leeds was to help Bates wring compensation out of Chelsea for luring away youth players. He said there was something impressively direct about Wise's first training session at Leeds, something he summarised as 'management'.

'I don't think personal [friendship] comes into it,' insisted Wise when asked if the fact that Bates was godfather to one of his children would spare him the sack. 'I know that one day it will happen, but Batesy will still be godfather to my son. There's a working relationship, and I trust him. If I do the job right, I won't get the sack, if I don't, I will, simple as that.'

No one else would have dared use the chummy 'Batesy'.

All the bonhomie and back-slapping cut no ice with the Leeds fans for whom Chelsea had always been hated foes. To see Bates filling the place with his cronies was anathema to the cloth cap brigade, who grew more and more worried about what it would do to their beloved club.

Wise could do little to change things in the short term and even though Leeds beat Southend in his first game, the team lost eight of the next twelve fixtures, ending 2006 second bottom and staring relegation squarely in the face.

Wise told Sean Gregan and Paul Butler to find other clubs and instructed Robbie Blake to lose weight, though he described the striker as a 'little gem' after his two goals helped Leeds beat Colchester.

'There's a lot of things wrong with this team and Gus and I know we've got to give them confidence,' he admitted. 'We need some fresh faces ... At the present moment trying to get them is very difficult. I was well aware of the job when I came here and it doesn't faze me too much to be honest. We know it's a difficult job, and we know these players are lacking a lot of confidence ... Bringing in new faces gives the place a lift and I think that is important. I think they've got into a rut, and I think now is the right time to bring some faces in to give competition ... People know they are going to play and it becomes a difficult situation when that happens. Too many players are in a comfort zone because of that situation. We want to make some changes, and we will make some changes at some point ... These players need to take a look at themselves, get together and dig us out of this hole because they are the players that are here at the moment.'

Wise furiously pilloried the unknown 'mole' who revealed his team selection to Crystal Palace, insisting he would never play for the club again, even though he could not identify the culprit.

He did what he could to strengthen, bringing in Casper Ankergren, Armando Sa, Robbie Elliott, Matt Heath, Alan Thompson, Tore Andre Flo, Rado Kishishev, Lubo Michalik and Tresor Kandol. The changes brought some improvement and there were victories against Luton, Preston and Plymouth in a five-game unbeaten run from 10 March to 7 April which brought hope that Wise could yet dig Leeds out of the hole.

The 2-1 defeat of Plymouth was crucial, the first time that Leeds had won two in a row all season. Michalik's header three minutes from time took United out of the bottom three for the first time since 25 November.

Easter Monday's trip to Colchester was massive. Leeds seemed to be on course to continue their revival when Eddie Lewis scored early in the second half, but Colchester fought back through Chris Iwelumo, who headed home a Karl Duguid free kick on eighty-two minutes. Jamie Cureton pounced in the last minute to condemn Leeds to defeat.

'They were poor goals to concede,' complained Wise, 'because we had looked comfortable ... We had a mad ten or twelve minutes where we didn't defend properly.'

The impact of the defeat was amplified by events elsewhere over that same ten-minute spell. Late strikes from Southend and QPR saw them convert draws into victories and Barnsley beat Birmingham to dump United back into the relegation zone.

Matt Heath's header was enough to beat Burnley five days later. It improved morale and brought Leeds level on points with Hull.

A week later, however, more late goals plunged Leeds further into the relegation morass. They lost at Southampton after conceding a goal six minutes from the end. They had to play almost an hour with ten men after

Thompson was wrongly sent off. The red card was rescinded but the damage had been done.

The same afternoon, Hull's injury-time goal at Stoke allowed the Tigers to secure a draw which took them a point clear of Leeds with two games remaining.

When Richard Cresswell opened the scoring in the penultimate game, at home to Ipswich on 28 April, it looked like Leeds might yet escape. But veteran Hull striker Dean Windass scored at Cardiff after fifty-two minutes and keeper Boaz Myhill kept the Bluebirds at bay to secure three points for Hull.

An Ipswich equaliser in the closing minutes ended United's hopes, three points in Hull's wake and with a vastly inferior goal difference. Hundreds of supporters flooded onto the pitch in an ill-advised attempt to get the game abandoned, but it was to no avail. After a delay of thirty minutes, play resumed and the final few seconds were played out. There were floods of tears and an outpouring of anger from the stands as Leeds' relegation to the third tier for the first time was confirmed.

In a symbolic farewell to the glory days, Gary Kelly came back onto the field when order was restored to receive a presentation to mark his retirement after 531 appearances over sixteen years with the club. United legends Paul Reaney, Allan Clarke, Mick Jones and Frank Worthington were on hand as Kelly was given a crystal cut vase to commemorate the occasion.

It provided a sad end to the saddest of afternoons, thirty-eight years to the day since United won their first league championship by drawing at Liverpool. By the time of the final game the following week at Derby, forty-four players including seventeen loanees had appeared for a team which had been captained by eight different men and lost twenty-six Championship games. The fall of Leeds United was complete.

CHAPTER TEN

Into the Abyss

With relegation confirmed, any penalty for entering administration became irrelevant. Ken Bates needed no prompting – reasoning that here was the means of clearing the soaring debt in one fell swoop, he held a board meeting on the Monday following the draw with Ipswich to discuss the financial position and next steps.

There was very little choice. At the end of March, the balance sheet creaked under a debt of £34.7 million, massively up from the £13.4 million of the previous June. It was estimated that a cash injection of £10 million was required just to continue trading and no one had a clue where the money was coming from.

That Monday afternoon, former chairman Gerald Krasner claimed, 'I'm 90 per cent sure that before next Tuesday Leeds will be in administration unless a white knight comes along in the meantime.' Things moved even more quickly than Krasner had thought.

Bates appointed accountants KPMG to advise the club and appointed them as administrators at 3.15 on Thursday 4 May.

He insisted that none of the problems were down to him, commenting snidely, 'The action taken brings to an end the financial legacy left by others that we have spent millions of pounds trying to settle. But the important thing now is not to view this as the end, but the beginning of a new era.'

His drastic action had been precipitated by the taxman. Among Leeds' debts was a historic liability to HMRC, which Bates had agreed to clear by monthly instalments of £200,000. Over the two years since his takeover, the club had repaid £5 million, including the clearance of £1.4 million in arrears in October 2006. Bates had sorted that with a settlement from Chelsea for tapping up two youth players. Another £2.6 million was due to be paid by 2008.

Money was so tight that the club defaulted on its instalments in March and April. That pushed HMRC over the edge and they served a winding-up petition on 17 April. The club had to clear the debt of £5 million by the end of June or face liquidation.

The Revenue viewed the matter as a test case. They had always bitterly resented the approach of the football authorities whereby players and clubs were treated as preferential creditors, reducing the money available for normal creditors like themselves. They had been agitating for change for years and saw United as the ideal victim against which to take a stand. A spokesman said, 'We are furious at the raw deal we have got out of this debacle. We are getting a penny in the pound for £7 million of public money which should be used to pay for hospitals and schools and other important public services.'

Over the previous year, Bates had been busily working away in the background to prepare for just such an eventuality. He had engineered various machinations involving organisations that could exploit the opaque confidentiality offered by tax havens. For a man as obstinate as Bates, it was almost a matter of honour to beat both the odds and the taxman.

Forward Sports Fund, formally the owners of Leeds United, was owed £2.4 million. There was a liability of £2.5 million to the Krato Trust (registered in Nevis), while the debt to Astor Investment Holdings (registered in the British Virgin Islands) was £12.8 million. All these sums related to funds advanced to United in 2005 and 2006.

At the end of March, Astor and Krato had threatened to withdraw ongoing support for the club and place it into liquidation unless security was granted in Astor's favour. The United board agreed to the request. Clearly it had been a ruse, but within a week Astor's loans were secured with a debenture, giving it a mortgage over club assets, preferential creditors by any other name.

Bates formed a new company, Leeds United Football Club Limited (LUFCL), solely for the purpose of buying the club from the administrators. Shortly after appointment, KPMG agreed to sell the business and assets to LUFCL, the directors of which were Bates, United chief executive Shaun Harvey and Mark Taylor, a close associate of Bates.

Krasner commented, 'The Bates deal is not a done deal because it has to be approved by creditors and I know of seven other consortiums who are interested in making a bid for Leeds. I must stress I'm not part of any of these consortiums. I have no financial interest in any of this.'

The purchase would be facilitated by the agreement of a Company Voluntary Arrangement (CVA), a legal transaction which would allow the debts to be settled at a discounted rate. A CVA required the support of 75 per cent of the creditors and Bates had saw to it that Forward, Krato and Astor had sufficient votes between them to satisfy this requirement.

Others accused him of trying to rig the vote – their cynicism appeared well-founded when all sorts of obscure liabilities were trotted out during the process, including £273,615 owed to Taylor's legal services company and £480,000 due to Yorkshire Radio, Bates' propaganda machine.

Conversely, the claims of parties opposed to Bates, including Krasner, Morris, Levi and Blackwell, were slashed. They put forward sums totalling £21.2 million but KPMG determined that the valid figure was £6.

On 14 May, KPMG's Stephen Fleming wrote to creditors informing them of a meeting to be held on 1 June. The letter included a full list of the £38 million owing to creditors. Astor, Forward and Krato were the biggest three, totalling £17.6 million, and gave their unqualified support for the Bates offer.

Fleming wrote, 'Creditors will be invited to vote on the proposal and any modifications that emerge. We know from preliminary discussions that the deal is supported by some of the larger creditors by value, however it still requires a majority of 75 per cent to be approved. If the proposal is carried, the CVA process will move forward, which will involve agreeing the club's new ownership with the Football League and paying a dividend to creditors.'

Krasner branded Bates' offer as 'utterly derisory … Mr Bates' new company is proposing a dividend of 1p in the pound. Effectively, he will have bought the club back debt-free for approximately £500,000, including professional costs.'

The Guardian reported that Astor was willing to write off £8 million to ensure that Bates retained control and would allow United to be bankrupted if the deal fell through. The newspaper and its investigative journalist David Conn had become a thorn in Bates' flesh with their pursuit of the truth. Their probing was so persistent that Bates later banned them from Elland Road in a fit of pique.

At the 1 June meeting, Fleming revealed that there had been six bids for the club, five from the UK and the other from a US-based group. The count of votes showed a total of 75.02 per cent in favour of the Bates deal.

KPMG adjourned the meeting and arranged for a recount to be held the following Monday. KPMG had disallowed a substantial number of creditor votes on both sides and it was reported that even if the recount confirmed the vote, Bates would face legal action.

KPMG announced that Bates' offer of 1p in the pound was the only acceptable deal on the table because it was the only one the largest creditor would support. With more than 25 per cent of the allowed debt, they could make or break any agreement – despite other offers on the table with a greater return for creditors, the club would face potential liquidation if Bates' deal was not accepted.

It was a position that many at the meeting found unpalatable. A series of searching questions were asked about links between Astor and Bates. If a link were established, it could have affected Astor's ability to vote on the grounds of a prejudicial interest.

KPMG had been unable to find any link despite 'extensive inquiries' – they accepted sworn statements from Bates and Taylor, plus a letter from Astor that they were not connected. It transpired that Leeds United's accounts included a reference to Astor having 'an interest in Forward Sports Fund' as of June 2006. The administrator admitted the link had not been spotted, but a brazen Taylor told the meeting, 'There was an association on 30 June – there isn't now.'

When KPMG were asked why the offshore entities should agree to write off millions of pounds in return for a sale to a new company in which they had no interest, Fleming said, 'Maybe they had football in their hearts and wanted the club to survive.' Bates could only 'presume' it was because Astor wanted to lend United more money.

And thereby hung the reason for the widespread criticism.

Krasner attempted to force an amendment to the deal which would compel Bates to remain at the helm of the club for more than five years or pay a penalty to creditors, but Astor blocked the move, meaning Bates could sell up after six months.

To grease the wheels, Taylor abruptly announced that Bates' deal would include a further £5 million for creditors if Leeds returned to the Premiership within five years. He admitted he had borrowed the idea from rival bidder Simon Morris. The sweetener was included in the final deal put to 1,350 creditors.

Morris increased his offer to 40p in the pound in a desperate late bid to block Bates, but KPMG ruled that the offer could not be put to creditors because the vote had already taken place.

The recount on the Monday confirmed Bates' success, his backing rising to 75.2 per cent. To allow any creditor time to dispute the decision in court, the club would remain in administration for a further twenty-eight days. *The Telegraph* reported that the Economic Secretary to the Treasury, Ed Balls, held a meeting with tax officials and MPs to discuss a possible challenge.

It had been expected that United's Football League share would be returned that week but the League insisted that they would not act until the CVA had been formally completed. They deferred consideration until their next board meeting on 12 July.

On 2 July, Bates upped the ante following a meeting between Leeds United officials, KPMG and HMRC. In an attempt to dissuade appeals, the offer of 1p in the pound was increased to 8p and the £5 million bonus for promotion to the top flight jumped from a timescale of five years to ten. The improved offer was conditional on there being no challenge to the transfer to Bates' new company. 'If the CVA is challenged,' commented Bates, 'the consequence will be liquidation, Leeds United will cease to exist and 500 jobs will be lost. It is our view that any challenge now will not be made on commercial grounds but is either politically or personally motivated.'

Just before the 4.00 p.m. deadline on 3 July, HMRC lodged a legal challenge. Its submission included a fifty-two-page witness statement questioning the voting rights of Krato, Astor and Forward and the administrator's decision as to the amount allowed to vote at the creditors meeting by Astor, Mark Taylor & Co. and Yorkshire Radio.

KPMG protested that it had been advised by two specialist insolvency barristers on the amounts that specific proxies should be allowed to vote for to ensure that the vote was conducted fairly, but their interpretation was widely condemned.

3 September was set as the date for the hearing of HMRC's challenge, three weeks after the start of the new season. KPMG feared that the judgement might not be handed down until October and even then could be subject to appeal. KPMG doubted that there were sufficient funds for the club to continue trading through to the conclusion of the process and 'concluded that embarking on such a process, which would put realisations available for creditors at risk, was not appropriate'.

KPMG reminded the creditors that the League's policy was that the football shares could only be transferred via a CVA other than in exceptional circumstances. KPMG had been told that a transfer under the exceptional circumstances provision had not taken place in any of the previous forty-five football club insolvencies and that such circumstances were undefined and entirely at the League's discretion.

Given that Astor had consistently stated it would vote against any CVA other than Bates' deal and had enough votes to block any CVA, KPMG concluded that a CVA proposing a sale to any other party would not be approved and issued an abort certificate to abandon the CVA.

KPMG then re-offered the club for sale on 6 July, inviting offers on an unconditional basis with a deadline of 5.00 p.m. on Monday 9 July.

Four offers were received by the deadline and considered by KPMG the following evening. They accepted Bates' revised bid and completed the transaction on 11 July.

It was a controversial decision, with the 'Astor impact' scuppering the other four bids. Bates' offer resulted in a dividend of 52.9p in the pound, with the next best offer at 32.2p. After removing the impact of Astor's favouritism towards Bates, his offer was reduced to 10.3p while both Offers B (13.2p) and C (15.7p) would pay more.

The matter was still not done. The Football League rejected United's request for the Football Share, expressing concern at KPMG's handling of the whole process and instructed chairman Lord Mawhinney to obtain legal advice on the matter. The decision had been taken at a board meeting on 12 July when KPMG had been expected to attend. They failed to do so and offered no explanation for their absence.

Bates insisted that documentation outstanding from KPMG had been forwarded to the League. 'The club are concerned that any issues the League board may have with the conduct of the administration process by KPMG should not affect the decision-making process as to the return of our share in the League and are seeking assurances from them on this point.'

United fans launched a protest against the whole dirty affair, laying flowers, scarves and shirts around the statue of Billy Bremner outside the Elland Road ground, with slogans calling for Bates to go. The following Saturday, fans stripped to the waist as they chanted 'Bates out' during the friendly defeat at Burnley. Removing their footwear, they added, 'Shoes off if you hate Ken Bates.' You could taste the animosity for the owner.

On 31 July, KPMG and representatives from United met with Lord Mawhinney for four hours in an attempt to reach agreement. Initially, the League denied that these were exceptional circumstances, a position strongly refuted by Bates. The League did not dispute that Bates' offer was the best one on the table but wanted it put to a new creditors' meeting. Because the players' wages had been paid and some players had left during the close season, the football creditors had reduced, meaning the Revenue's votes as a proportion of the whole had increased. KPMG were of the view that the Revenue now represented 24.4 per cent of the debt and could block any CVA.

It was agreed to approach the Revenue to persuade them to withdraw their objection. They categorically insisted that as a matter of policy, they would vote against any CVA that saw football creditors paid in full. If the CVA was passed, they would appeal again and would litigate all the way.

Given this stance, KPMG said a further meeting was futile.

David Hartnett, the second most powerful official at HMRC, insisted that Leeds must pay the £7.7 million owed in tax but on 30 August, HMRC formally withdrew their legal challenge. A spokeswoman said it had become academic when the CVA was ditched in early July. She would not be drawn on why it had taken the Revenue nearly two months to formally kill off the case and nor would she elaborate on what steps the taxman would take to recover the debt.

The impasse was broken on 2 August with the League board agreeing to transfer the League Share under the exceptional circumstances provision. There was a sting in the tail, however.

The League's statement added, 'It is acknowledged the club did go into administration and has been unable to comply with the terms of the League's well-established Insolvency Policy. As a result, the board determined this transfer of membership should be subject to Leeds United having a fifteen-point deduction applicable from the beginning of the 2007/08 season.'

It was said that the League had considered demoting United to League Two as an alternative, but the 'lighter penalty' was like a red rag to Bates, who wrote to the chairmen of the other seventy-one League clubs on 8 August. He insisted that administration was 'not pre-planned. My staff at Leeds fought tooth and nail to get Leeds through to the start of the coming season ... We had procured external funding of approaching £25 million in our attempts to keep the club alive. We spent nine months looking for external partners but as our playing fortunes declined during last season investors waited to see what would happen and this combined with falling gate receipts meant that by the end of the season funding had run out. We had paid HMRC some £5 million during the period from January 2005 to April 2007 but the Revenue would not allow us more time to pay the outstanding arrears ... Administration or liquidation was really the only option.

'We have attracted some criticism for going into administration before the end of the 2006/07 season, and thus triggering the ten-point deduction during that season when we were almost certain of relegation. I think this criticism is unfair. Lord Mawhinney has stated publicly that the approach we took was completely within the rules. As directors of the club, we had a duty to act in the best interests of the club and we believe that in taking the actions we did we discharged our obligations properly. The supporters of Leeds United would have rightly been appalled if we had been relegated and then have taken a ten-point deduction that could have been taken during the 2006/07 season.'

Despite Bates' protests, more than 75 per cent of the chairmen voted in favour of the punishment. He was incandescent, pointing out the obvious conflict of interest and, while Dennis Wise pressed ahead with plans for the new season, Bates pledged to overturn the decision.

United representatives wrote to the FA requesting a review of the case, insisting the appeal should have been heard by an independent panel. On 27 September, the FA informed the club that they did not believe it appropriate for there to be any further inquiry.

In October, United wrote to the FA drawing its attention to inconsistencies in the FA's decision and asked them to look at it again. This request was rejected by the FA's director of corporate affairs, the same person who rejected the original request. United complained about a lack of impartiality.

On 27 November, FA officials confirmed they would not initiate an independent investigation into the matter. United wrote back inviting the

FA to waive their right that the dispute should be determined through their arbitration procedures and allow the matter to be referred directly to the High Court for a Judicial Review. If they refused this request, United would 'commence independent arbitration proceedings in accordance with FA regulations'.

Three weeks later, United wrote to the FA again to request that the matter be referred to an Independent Arbitration Tribunal. They also requested that the hearing should take place in public.

In February, spooked by the idea of its dirty laundry being washed in public, the League invited United to arbitration rather than a High Court case. Under duress, United agreed.

A start date of 15 April was agreed for the hearing. The tribunal's ruling was expected to be made public before United's League One fixture at Millwall on 19 April, the third last game of the season.

After several delays, it was announced on 1 May that United's appeal had been rejected. The legal challenge failed when it was proved Mark Taylor had signed to accept the penalty and agreed not to mount a legal challenge. Bates claimed the outcome as a moral victory and called on Lord Mawhinney and the League board to resign before loudly harrumphing, 'If this is justice, I am a banana.'

CHAPTER ELEVEN

Fifteen Points, We Don't Give a F***!

So crippling was the wrangling that followed Ken Bates' decision to plunge Leeds into administration, that it would be difficult to imagine how preparations for the new season could have been worse. At a time when the Elland Road club desperately needed to pull together, it was in grave danger of falling apart completely.

As if contemplating a first ever campaign in English football's third tier wasn't bad enough, there was a multitude of barriers put in the way. The club was barred from signing any new players until the first week of August when it was finally granted the League Share.

A number of players were sold when United began trading, with David Healy to Fulham, Richard Cresswell to Stoke City, Kevin Nicholls to Preston North End and Robbie Blake to Burnley the biggest names, though young starlet Danny Rose moved to Tottenham for £1 million.

When United received clearance to start signing players, they quickly took advantage. Alan Thompson, Casper Ankergren, Tore Andre Flo and Matt Heath all made short contracts or loan deals permanent. Several players were still under contract, including Frazer Richardson, Eddie Lewis, Rui Marques, Jermaine Beckford, Jonathan Douglas, Ian Westlake, Jonny Howson, Gylfi Einarsson, Seb Carole, Tresor Kandol and Shaun Derry. There were new arrivals in the shape of Leon Constantine, Curtis Weston, David Prutton and Andy Hughes as Dennis Wise assembled something resembling a first-team squad.

With the clear-out of United's big-name strikers and Constantine and Flo injured, much would depend on Kandol and Beckford. Wise, impressed by Beckford in pre-season, expected great things of him.

Asked about the points penalty, Wise said, 'Not only have they taken my arms and legs off, now they've cut my balls off as well. It's just not funny at all. I'm disappointed with the whole thing. Minus fifteen points. We have to get 106 points to win the league, ninety-two points to get in the play-offs and seventy points to stay up. Lovely. Thank you very much.'

Wise and Poyet turned the sanction to the club's advantage. They built a siege mentality with players and fans united in their paranoid opposition to the Football League as Ken Bates kept his head down. The tactics worked splendidly and Leeds won their first seven games, quickly wiping out the fifteen-point penalty, thanks in the main to the goals of Kandol and Beckford.

There was an ugly altercation when United met Luton, now managed by Kevin Blackwell, at Elland Road on 1 September. Leeds won a tight game by the only goal. It might have been the result, or bitterness at the way he was sacked by the club, but a furious Blackwell got so close to Wise that the men's foreheads touched briefly.

Wise remained calm throughout the confrontation, refusing to bite, but said afterwards, 'I don't think Kevin wanted to shake my hand. He told me to F-off ... The emotion was very high, but if you don't get the result you want, you don't spit your dummy out in front of everyone.'

Leeds' opening spurt was devastating, all the more astonishing as the team had yet to hit full stride. They had been carried forward on a wave of righteous indignation, determined to exact revenge on the Football League, but at times the luck had gone their way. Nevertheless, it was difficult to argue with a goals record of sixteen for and just three against.

Just as fans started to believe that United would sweep all before them, there was a nasty shock, away to relegation-threatened Gillingham.

Things looked good after Seb Carole's goal just before the half-hour – Beckford had already had an effort chalked off for offside and it seemed Leeds would just steamroller their way on.

Kandol was booked two minutes before the goal for protesting that he had been fouled, and five minutes before the break he was shown the red card for sarcastically applauding when referee Danny McDermid awarded him a free kick.

United continued to look good with Beckford playing alone up front but he was booked for chipping the ball past the keeper after the whistle had gone for offside. Beckford was fouled a few minutes later by Sodje, who had been involved in Kandol's dismissal and had been relentless in his challenges. The referee awarded the free kick without cautioning the defender. However, when Beckford challenged Sean Clohessy, the red card was waved and United were down to nine men.

Wise immediately made a double substitution, introducing Huntington and Westlake in place of Clapham and Hughes. The latter had already been booked and Wise couldn't afford to lose anyone else. Douglas was next to see yellow after Gillingham's Graham fouled Carole and escaped with only a free kick. On sixty-eight minutes Ankergren was cautioned for reasons unclear, and the game threatened to descend into farce.

United, still ahead, set out their stall to defend the lead. They almost made it but conceded in the first minute of injury-time. Veteran Neil Cox rose to nod home a corner and a remarkable run was over.

United bounced back with victory at Brighton on 20 October. The three points left them ninth in the table, just six points off top spot – when they beat Millwall 4-2 a week later they were in the play-off positions after thirteen games. It was an astonishing achievement.

However, matters off the field now took a hand.

Down in London, Tottenham Hotspur had appointed Juande Ramos as coach. When they sought to appoint a number two, it was an open secret that Gus Poyet topped their list of candidates. There was minimal resistance from Elland Road but the Uruguayan's absence was badly felt as the team's form slumped.

United's first challenge following Poyet's departure was a visit to table-topping Carlisle on 3 November. The Cumbrians' biggest crowd for more than thirty years flocked into Brunton Park to witness the game.

It looked like the juggernaut would go rolling on when Beckford put United ahead after twenty-eight minutes with a tap in, but the home side came storming back over the last half-hour. Simon Hackney powered home a half-volley from 25 yards and nine minutes later Joe Garner nodded home at the near post to put Carlisle ahead.

It had been one of Leeds' finest performances of the season, but Carlisle had the impetus. It was evident the thirteen-game unbeaten run was over long before Bridge-Wilkinson hit a third goal in the fourth minute of stoppage time.

United responded to the reverse with a midweek win at Bournemouth, but then slumped badly, struggling to beat Swindon and then losing to Hereford in an FA Cup replay. Worse still, they were undone by a single goal four minutes from time at Cheltenham, rooted to the bottom of the table with only two wins.

United were still fifth and on course for promotion, but they had suffered four defeats in seven games. The collapse corresponded exactly with the departure of Poyet.

Just as it seemed the train was coming off the rails, Leeds halted their slump with two impressive home wins, 3-0 against Port Vale and 4-0 over Huddersfield. Beckford got three of the goals and Flo two as United left themselves just a couple of points off top spot.

United had to rely on an injury-time goal from a 25-yard Alan Thompson free kick to snatch a draw at Walsall on 15 December. Jonathan Douglas twisted his knee in the closing minutes and was likely to be sidelined for three months. On Boxing Day, Beckford got a goal in the closing seconds at Hartlepool to snatch a 1-1 draw.

A five-game unbeaten run came to an end three days later when Leeds visited pace setters Swansea.

The Welshmen opened the scoring in the ninth minute but Beckford quickly equalised. Garry Monk headed Swansea into the lead, but they were down to ten men when Ferrie Bodde was sent off for a foul on Jonny Howson seven minutes before the break. It didn't faze them and they went 3-1 ahead on the stroke of half-time.

United were back in it when Thompson scored from a free kick a minute after the resumption and he hit the post from another set piece moments later, but Leeds could not fashion a comeback and lost 3-2.

It was a disappointing way to end the year, but there is no doubt that Wise would have taken third place had he been offered it at the start of the season.

However, he was not around to finish the job he had started – on 28 January it was reported that he had agreed to join Newcastle as director of football.

Wise had shown the testy side of his personality with some increasingly irritable reactions as United's form began to dip. He had grown disenchanted with life at Elland Road since the departure of Poyet and was understood to want a change of pace from the day-to-day grind of football management. Newcastle would allow him to spend just a few days a week on Tyneside, with the rest in London.

The move came out of the blue and devastated Ken Bates. He had ignored a speculative article in the *Mail on Sunday* but then received a call to say Newcastle had asked for permission to speak to Wise. Bates demanded confirmation in writing that they would pay compensation before he would allow any discussion to take place.

Wise had a one-year rolling contract, and if either party broke it, they would have to compensate the other. Wise was adamant that he wanted to take Newcastle up on their offer. He apologised that it was such short notice, but it was too good an opportunity to miss.

'We've agreed that he will prepare the team for tomorrow,' said Bates, 'but it wouldn't be appropriate if he was at the game. He will get them ready for the game and hopefully he will go out on a high.'

There were other intrigues involving Newcastle at the time with strong rumours that their former chairman Freddy Shepherd was ready to invest in 'a northern club' with Leeds said to be his primary target.

Shepherd banked more than £37 million when he sold his stock in Newcastle to businessman Mike Ashley. 'Football's a drug, and a powerful drug,' said Shepherd. 'From January I think something could happen.'

Bates underlined his determination to take Leeds back into the Premier League. 'There are plenty of would-be investors sniffing round Leeds United,' he admitted. 'It could be tempting to take the money and run. Let me assure you, that possibility is not even in the mind of Suzannah and myself. We are here to build not just Yorkshire's number one club, but one which will compete and take on the so-called greats.'

Bates made no secret of the fact that Shepherd could be an 'ideal partner'; the pair had formed a good friendship thanks to their work in football.

The rumours first surfaced in September when Shepherd was spotted dining with Bates in the North East. At the time, Bates said, 'Freddy is a good friend of mine and has been for years. I went up to see him, and we finished up having lunch. Inevitably the subject of football came out, and he is still a bit sore about what happened at Newcastle. He would like to get back in and I would like an investor, so the two fit in.'

Shepherd wanted at least a 25 per cent stake to make his investment worthwhile, but Bates was clear he would maintain a majority. His takeover in the summer included an 'anti-embarrassment clause' which stated that 50 per cent of any takeover fee above £5 million would be shared among the club's creditors. The clause would remain in place until the summer of 2008.

Bates wrote in his matchday column, 'For the avoidance of doubt, Leeds United is not for sale and any tentative enquiries on that front have been rebuffed. It is no secret that we will welcome a serious substantial partner. Note the word is "welcome" – not "need". We are progressing very well on the road to recovery but we recognise that an injection of capital would accelerate the process.'

CHAPTER TWELVE

Return of the Mac

'When I was first approached, I couldn't quite believe it. It's a great honour to be back at the club and I can't wait to get in and amongst it.'

Former Leeds midfielder Gary McAllister had the broadest grin imaginable as he spoke to the press after his appointment as Leeds United manager.

There was an instant connect between the fans and a man who had been at the heart of United's midfield when the club won the league championship in 1992. An elegant playmaker, he made almost 300 appearances in six years and won fifty-seven caps for Scotland.

'When a new manager is appointed late in January,' continued McAllister, 'it's usually to pick up the pieces of failure, but this is different. The boys are in a fantastic position, they can go second tonight ... From outside Yorkshire everyone has been amazed at what's been happening at Elland Road. You have to give credit to Dennis and the players for that. Now we have to get back focused for the real target and that's getting out of this league.'

There was no hiding McAllister's pleasure. He had been out of the game since resigning as Coventry manager in 2004 to care for his late wife as she battled cancer. He had feared he would never get another chance and he was delighted to return to a place he still considered his spiritual home.

A relationship with Bates was not something that sat particularly easily with the Scot, though he claimed it was 'very friendly'. Bates for his part was delighted, seeing it as a means of currying favour with the fans. They saw through that little ruse, although they welcomed McAllister back with open arms, relieved to see the back of Wise, a man to whom they had never warmed.

'A siege mentality can be a good thing, but you can't live like that for ever ... We have a duty to try and promote good football and help players play the game properly,' said McAllister, who maintained he wanted promotion without having to resort to kick-and-rush or cynical gamesmanship. 'I absolutely believe that you can play passing football in League One.

'It's been a total blur ... It took me two seconds to accept the offer. The lure of this club is so great I couldn't even begin to think about turning it down. It was a chance to help Leeds get back to where they should be.'

The early signs were not encouraging. McAllister's first game saw United slip out of the play-off positions after losing at home to Tranmere. Three draws followed, extending United's winless run to seven.

'There's so much to play for, and that's what I'm trying to express to these guys,' said a frustrated McAllister. 'There's so much at stake for this club. We're going into the last third of the season, and we need people with character to really push it on ... We've got thirteen games left now, and we need points. Dropping points at home is not going to get us where we want to be. I'm seeing signs of improvement, but ultimately it doesn't matter what happens at the training ground or what we see during the week. It's what people can produce on matchday.'

The problem was easy to spot, the goals had dried up. McAllister's first victory came on 1 March, courtesy of Kandol's goal at Swindon, his second since the beginning of November – Beckford had managed two goals in two months.

The manager approached Crystal Palace to test out their willingness to release Scottish striker Dougie Freedman, but the player initially ruled out a move. After a change of heart, he joined Leeds on 7 March, on loan until the end of the season.

New Palace manager Neil Warnock warned Freedman he was unlikely to get many opportunities at Selhurst Park and the player commented, 'I'm still very much in love with the club and this is maybe the only way I can get back to playing there ... This is an opportunity to go and play some football, try to score a few goals, and try to get promotion for Leeds.'

First United goals for midfielders Bradley Johnson and Neil Kilkenny, both newly arrived in the transfer window, secured victory against Bournemouth, but then came an inexplicable defeat at home to Cheltenham. Freedman came on as sub in both games and showed his class. He scored twice on his first start on 15 March at Port Vale and impressed with the intelligence of his football. He shaped United's play, combining well with Beckford.

Unfortunately, United were off colour as a combination, allowing Vale to come back from two down at the break to draw level with goals just after the hour. Freedman's second, with four minutes remaining, looked to have sealed victory, but Luke Rodgers snatched an equaliser in the third minute of injury-time to leave McAllister bemoaning defensive fallibility.

The result saw Leeds slip to tenth, two points outside the play-offs. After just two wins from eleven, they faced a crucial run of five games against teams in the promotion shake up.

Return of the Mac

United were back to their best in beating Walsall 2-0 on 22 March. The goals, one in each half, both came from sharp Beckford finishes following killer through balls from Kilkenny. To round off a fine night, captain Jonathan Douglas came off the bench to complete his recovery from the injury he sustained before Christmas.

A week later Brighton came away from Elland Road with a goalless draw, but Leeds snapped back to win at Doncaster courtesy of Alan Sheehan's glorious free kick into the top corner. It was a bittersweet day for Sheehan whose yellow card was his tenth of the season, resulting in a two-game ban.

Victory at Leyton Orient restored Leeds to the play-off positions. The decisive second goal came from Beckford, who thus became the first United player to notch twenty in a season since Mark Viduka in 2003. Leeds reinforced their position by beating second-placed Carlisle at home with Freedman scoring twice. The improving fortunes saw Ken Bates reward McAllister with a twelve-month rolling contract.

At Yeovil on 25 April, a Freedman goal after four minutes secured victory and a play-off place, though the dismissal of Sheehan would see him miss out.

Leeds were paired with Carlisle, who had held runners-up spot from 22 March until 19 April before promotion jitters saw them slide to fourth.

United had home advantage in the first leg but failed to make it count. They created enough chances to win the game but were denied by an inspired display from Carlisle keeper Keiren Westwood.

Carlisle took the lead after thirty-two minutes when Simon Hackney's long-range effort was deflected in off the backside of Danny Graham.

Five minutes after the resumption, Carlisle broke away and combined cleverly to provide Marc Bridge-Wilkinson with the chance to increase the lead. His confident finish as he slid in at the centre of the box looked to have settled the contest.

After fifty-eight minutes, McAllister withdrew Beckford, suffering with an injured ankle, and introduced Kandol, but the move was roundly jeered. The tall target man did little, apart from one long-range drive that was almost as high as it was wide.

McAllister was contemplating having to climb a mountain in Cumbria as the match ticked into its fifth minute of injury-time. Then Lady Luck smiled on his charges – Kandol's lumbering presence unsettled the Carlisle defence when a long punt forward from Paul Huntington fell into the heart of their penalty area. Freedman swept the loose ball home to give United a glimmer of hope and sent the Leeds fans away with something to remember.

Carlisle were widely regarded as bankers for the second leg but their confidence was shaken when Leeds opened the scoring after ten minutes.

Ankergren's long goal kick drifted across to Prutton, who nodded on to Beckford. He challenged for the dropping ball and flicked on to Jonny Howson, bursting through from midfield. Howson played it wide to Freedman on the left and took the return, chested it on and slotted home left-footed to bring Leeds back on level terms. It was a hammer blow to Carlisle.

The goal settled Leeds and sent anxieties coursing through the Carlisle veins. Bridge-Wilkinson had been a real thorn in the United flesh at Elland Road, but he was never allowed to exercise the same degree of influence in the second leg and Hackney was rendered a passenger on the left flank. Carlisle's supply line was snuffed out by a Leeds midfield that erased the memory of their dismal first leg display, though the game seemed set for extra-time.

Referee Alan Wiley had signalled there would be one minute of injury-time at the end as United picked up a loose ball and started to play their way through midfield. Kilkenny fed Freedman, who laid it off to Howson. The young midfielder shifted it into space and then clipped a shot back towards the bottom corner. The keeper, seeing it late, could not react as the ball ran on inside the post to put United ahead.

The players rushed to congratulate an overjoyed Howson as the fans went wild.

Carlisle had time to restart the game, though there was little conviction in their long ball forward. Ankergren claimed it calmly and United played out the remaining forty-one seconds to secure a memorable victory.

McAllister paid tribute to the Leeds supporters. 'I know what 40,000 of them sound like ... That was for them tonight. The players would be first to admit that. It was a bit of a damp squib on Monday night at Elland Road, but I think the fans got the reaction they wanted.'

A Doncaster team widely regarded as the best footballing side in League One were Leeds' opponents in the final, United's first appearance at the new Wembley Stadium. Rovers had earned a reputation for neat possession and a wonderful passing game, but Leeds were favourites, determined to make history as the first United side to win a play-off final after unsuccessful attempts in 1987 and 2006.

United's fans heavily outnumbered those of Rovers. They had a 10,000 advantage and made themselves heard when Football League chairman Lord Mawhinney came out to be introduced to the players before kick-off. The chorus of whistles, boos and jeers was ear-shattering as he went along the lines with a fixed grin.

Leeds kicked off to tumultuous cheering but could easily have been out of it in the first fifteen minutes. Doncaster's players were sharp, quickly getting their short passing movements going and picked holes in the United rearguard.

A smart interpassing combination in the area nearly put Price in and then Ankergren had to save one-handed at the feet of Coppinger. A minute later the keeper saved United again as Hayter was allowed to run clear on the left with the back four appealing for offside. Ankergren was called into action again in the twelfth minute as Hayter moved through on their right.

The Danish goalkeeper was giving a great exhibition, his saves in that opening quarter of an hour marking him out as man of the match.

United couldn't find a way out of their own half in the opening minutes – they started to find some of their long passing across the defence and midfield but as soon as they tried to make more aggressive forays into the Doncaster half, the Rovers defence easily swallowed the ball.

McAllister spent the interval encouraging United to keep up the football, but he should have saved his breath. Almost instantly, his men let Doncaster in.

In the first ten seconds, Michalik sent Stock crashing to the ground as he made his way to the edge of United's area. Coppinger's free kick was blocked and the follow-up was deflected for a corner. Rovers made the most of it, an unmarked Hayter diving to head home the dropping ball with Ankergren and Kilkenny unable to get in a block. United were behind with ninety seconds of the half gone.

McAllister feared the worst. Doncaster had the perfect containing game, setting up two banks of four and retaining possession. Leeds, as so often over the years, could not find their form when it mattered most. They lacked the penetration to find the chinks in the final third and their attacks were laboured.

The arrival of Kandol from the bench led to some route one football and goalmouth scrambles, but the blunderbuss misfired. Former Leeds keeper Neil Sullivan was faultless in his handling and composed under pressure – there was too much anxiety about the United thrusts as time slipped away. They either ran up blind alleys or made life easy for Sullivan with aimless high balls.

United's best chance came after eighty-five minutes when Michalik's presence in the area caused panic from a throw. The ball ran out to Douglas who sailed into a fierce shot, only to see it swing narrowly wide of Sullivan's left-hand post.

And that was that – United were condemned to a second year in League One.

Determined to make up for the disappointment, Bates and McAllister went for it in the summer, persuading Swansea wide man Andy Robinson to forsake the certainty of Championship football. He was soon joined by towering Bristol City striker Enoch Showunmi, Livingstone winger Rob Snodgrass and Argentine forward Luciano Becchio.

The manager spoke of his hopes. 'This coming season is the first time this club has been able to look forward in many, many years ... I want the players to have the same mindset as last season ... They utilised the points deduction in making it a case of "we are Leeds, no one likes us but we just don't care." It was a siege mentality. It has to be the same again. Everything is in place in terms of our facilities and our crowd. There is no doubt in my mind that Leeds United will get back in the Premier League, it is just a matter of when.'

There wasn't the all-conquering start of 2007, but August and September went well, with five League One victories from eight games taking them third. There was also a decent Carling Cup run, including a 4-0 hammering of Championship side Crystal Palace.

McAllister unearthed a gem in teenage midfielder Fabian Delph whose succession of fine displays brought unwelcome attention from other clubs. United were quick to secure his future, tying him down to a four-year deal.

Everything seemed to be going well. The club announced that in the fourteen months to June they had made a profit of £4.5 million on turnover of £23.2 million, with an operating profit before player trading of £902,000.

But then the wheels came off. Leeds had lost three games out of five when they travelled to non-league Histon in the FA Cup on 30 November. On a filthy day in Cambridgeshire, they were made to look distinctly average on a mudbath of a pitch. The day was lost to a headed goal from centre-back Matthew Langston, a postman by day.

The media made the most of another bad day for Leeds and a bedraggled McAllister wondered out loud whether the players 'know the importance of this result ... We are a Third Division side and we played like one at times today.'

The three successive defeats which followed sent Leeds plunging to ninth, five points out of the play-off positions as McAllister's world collapsed around him.

United's desperate defensive problems were highlighted when McAllister brought in obscure French defender Mansour Assoumani. 'He's played in France and Germany so he's got some good experience and, as he can play at right-back as well as in the middle, he will give us more strength in the back four area,' said McAllister. It all sounded good but Assoumani's worth and reputation was overrated. Siegen terminated his contract in August, just before they kicked off in the fifth tier of German football.

His only appearance for Leeds came in a 3-1 defeat at MK Dons on 20 December and he was released a month later. The Dons result did for

McAllister, the fragility of his team exposed by their concession of two goals inside the first seventeen minutes – Leeds appeared liable to concede whenever MK Dons turned the screw.

United were fifteen points behind Leicester and eleven behind second-placed MK. It would take some revival to overturn such margins.

'It's not my decision, but I feel that I'm the guy who can take this club into the Championship,' said McAllister pathetically. He never got the opportunity. Bates swung the axe four days before Christmas.

CHAPTER THIRTEEN
Simon Grayson

Ken Bates did not dally over his third managerial appointment in two years. The day after the announcement of Gary McAllister's sacking, Blackpool furiously rejected United's request to speak to Pool manager Simon Grayson. Chairman Karl Oyston was livid at the way that Bates went about things and told Leeds so.

There had been a 'flood of bets' on Grayson, who was duly appointed to the Elland Road hot seat on 23 December, despite a threat of legal action by Oyston.

It was clear that Grayson was desperate to take the reins, saying, 'It's a massive club and it's close to my heart, having played here and supporting the club ... Hopefully, the fans will embrace what we are trying to do and we can grasp this opportunity to get the club back where it should be.

'When I first came as a fourteen-year-old I never thought I'd get to this stage, but as time goes by you get into the coaching side and this is one club I have always wanted to manage. I'd like to thank the chairman for giving me the opportunity to come into the club and hopefully it will be a successful partnership.'

The fit between Grayson and Bates was good – the two men gelled well from the start despite all Bates' idiosyncrasies.

Grayson's debut brought an impressive display against table-topping Leicester City. A revitalised Leeds threatened victory but had to settle for a draw. Grayson coaxed the players into delivering four wins from the next five games as Leeds climbed to seventh, their defence immeasurably bolstered by the arrival of Ipswich's Richard Naylor, a self-confessed Leeds nut.

A promising start was disrupted by the three-game suspension of Jermaine Beckford following a retrospective red card for violent conduct during the victory against Millwall.

Beckford, who scored both goals, was captured by TV cameras elbowing keeper David Forde in the face. He was cautioned on the night for a push and the FA gleefully handed out the ban for the elbow which it found that referee Alan Wiley had missed.

Without their talisman, Leeds lost poorly at Huddersfield and when they went down at Hereford frustrated supporters chanted, 'We're sh*t and we're sick of it.' Grayson was appalled by the nature of the defeat and held a post-match inquest in the cramped dressing room, telling the players exactly what he thought of them.

Grayson: 'When you hear your own fans singing things like that at the end of the game then the players should be hurting ... We've got to use this result as an example or an inspiration between now and the end of the season ... I'm not going to criticise individual players because that's not my style but we've had words in there ... One or two might not play for the club again.'

Months later, Grayson recalled, 'There are defining moments in any season and that was certainly one for us. The criticism they got from the fans was justified. The meeting that we had afterwards as a group ... really focused us on what we needed to do. We knew that after that game the players could either sink or swim ... It was a big game in our season.'

Grayson's words had the desired effect – Leeds went on an eleven-game unbeaten run that ushered them back up to fifth and odds-on for a play-off place with four games left. Their home form was ultra-impressive, nine straight wins with seven clean sheets.

Defeat at champions designate Leicester on 13 April was a blow but Leeds saw out the campaign with three straight victories to secure fourth place and qualification for the play-offs.

Leeds gave a determined defensive display at Millwall in the first leg of the semi-final. They thwarted the home side in the first half with Sam Sodje a key contributor to their defiance. The Nigerian international had become a cult hero since his loan move from Reading at the end of March.

Millwall's persistence got its reward in the seventy-second minute when Richard Naylor, who had given a tremendous display, misjudged the bounce as he dived to head clear a low cross. It looped on to Neil Harris, who controlled and evaded the challenge of Douglas, firing past Ankergren into the bottom corner. Exuberant Millwall fans poured onto the pitch and Ankergren was roughly manhandled.

Leeds could find no response and returned to Yorkshire empty-handed.

The spirit remained strong and Elland Road was an equally passionate cauldron of noise for the second leg as the players rose to the occasion. Millwall were on perpetual defence but Leeds struggled to fashion a clear opening. They were handed a real opportunity at the start of the second half when a penalty was awarded for a foul on Sodje.

Beckford fluffed his lines, scuffing a strike that the keeper gratefully saved.

No real damage was done – Leeds scored five minutes later, Becchio prodding home after Ben Parker topped off his storming run down the left with a tempting low cross.

That should have been enough to inspire Leeds but they were caught out badly by a sucker punch from Millwall after seventy-four minutes. From a rare breakaway, winger David Martin lofted a cross beyond the back post. Lewis Grabban cut it back to the centre of the 6-yard area where Jimmy Abdou was on hand to slip the ball home.

Leeds were done and couldn't find a way back at the end of a tiring season.

Simon Grayson refused to criticise the players, focusing instead on the extraordinary contribution from the fans. 'The support was unbelievable yet again and I can't thank them enough. The reception at the end meant a lot. Since the day I walked through the door in December, the fans have been with us every step of the way. I think the fans appreciate what we've done as a group, and that's how we will do it next year by all sticking together as a group. The fans knew we'd had a go at it … I'm more disappointed that we couldn't reward them, but we'll all come back stronger.'

Another season had ended in anticlimax, but there was a genuine feeling among the Elland Road faithful that United finally had the right man in the manager's chair. They were convinced that Grayson would deliver Championship football without the need to suffer the nerve-jangling lottery of the play-offs.

Ken Bates couldn't resist Aston Villa's £7.5 million offer for Fabian Delph in the summer but rejected a series of bids for Jermaine Beckford when the striker refused to sign a new three-year contract. There was plenty of interest from other clubs but no one would match United's asking price of £2.5 million. Bates and Grayson agreed that Beckford should be allowed to run his contract down and leave for nothing at the end of the season – if Leeds could get one last decent campaign out of him, his goals would be crucial in a promotion chase.

Their resistance paid off with Leeds getting away like a house on fire, outmatching even the strong starts of the previous two seasons. There was a single defeat and thirteen clean sheets in the first twenty-four games.

A 4-2 victory at Stockport on 28 December saw Leeds eight points clear of the chasing pack with eleven points in hand on third-placed Norwich. It looked like they would succeed at the third time of asking.

During their devastating run, Leeds successfully negotiated two rounds of the FA Cup to secure a money-spinning third-round clash with old rivals Manchester United at Old Trafford on 3 January.

Perhaps with a touch of his customary mind games, Reds boss Sir Alex Ferguson chose to talk up Leeds in the days leading up to the match, expressing admiration for their resurgence under Grayson.

'Simon's done a fantastic job ... He's got great motivation and his team aren't letting him down. They're playing really well at the moment. They won't be too far away from the Premier League in the next couple of years. With the position they're in it looks as if they're absolute certainties to be in the Championship next year.'

Recalling the time he once got stuck in his car at traffic lights near Elland Road, Ferguson recalled, 'This bunch of supporters, skinheads, twenty or thirty of them, see me and go "Ferguson!" and start running across the road. The lights are still red, I'm almost sh*tting myself, they're getting nearer, then the light goes to amber and [impersonation of a tyre squeal] I'm away.'

Ferguson named a strong eleven, including Wayne Rooney, and was clearly desperate for victory.

If Rooney and Co. expected an easy afternoon, they were rapidly disabused of the notion with Leeds on top-note from the start, playing controlled football with neat passing.

From somewhere in the ether, Leeds conjured a goal after eighteen minutes which the Elland Road faithful would remember for ever.

From a tussle deep in the Leeds half, Jonny Howson came away with the ball and broke into space. He got his head up and looked forward, spying Beckford at halfway with only Wes Brown alongside him. One touch to steady himself and BOOM! Howson sent the ball soaring 50 yards towards the Manchester box.

Beckford had a yard on Brown and put on the striker's burn to leave him in his wake. His attempt to cushion the ball on his thigh was poor and the ball ran wide to Beckford's left as Brown and goalkeeper Tomasz Kuszczak closed. Beckford calmly clipped the ball left-footed wide of the advancing keeper's reach to send it skimming in at the far post. It was a fine example of the goal-scorer's art.

Old Trafford was instantly alive with the baying celebrations of Leeds fans. Grayson demanded cool heads but the game also required fire and spirit and Naylor and Kisnorbo marshalled a stern rearguard action – they gave nothing to their illustrious hosts, securing a clenched-fist victory that would last long in the memory.

'We had 9,000 supporters there,' enthused Grayson. 'I remember walking down the side of the pitch to go to the press area at the end of the game, and they were all still there. Our head of media was walking really quickly and I said, "Slow down – we might never be part of this again, so let's enjoy listening to them." Before that, all the headlines about Leeds had been negative things. That put us back in the spotlight for the right reason.'

Bizarrely, the triumph destabilised Leeds. They could only draw at home to lowly Wycombe and then lost at Exeter as their advantage at the top began to crumble.

Their attention continued to be distracted by the Cup, the draw taking them to White Hart Lane to face Spurs.

Earlier in the day, Norwich's 1-0 defeat of Brentford had seen the Canaries usurp the League One leadership that United had monopolised since 19 September.

Tottenham were determined not to go the same way as Manchester United and manager Harry Redknapp instructed his men to pressurise Leeds from the off. His players took him at his word and the first twenty minutes saw Leeds penned into deep defence.

United were intent on making themselves difficult to break down, crowding Tottenham's midfielders and snapping into tackles before the home men could settle on the ball. Referee Alan Wiley had to call Snodgrass and Jermaine Jenas together for some calming words after one ill-tempered incident.

Nevertheless, Tottenham looked certain to secure the early goal they sought. After eight minutes, Gareth Bale's long throw into the area was nodded down by the towering Peter Crouch. Danny Rose got to it, but Michael Doyle came clattering into him with his foot up as he flicked the ball away. It was a clumsy challenge and the referee's penalty award was a simple decision.

Defoe was entrusted with the spot kick, and side-footed a low strike but it was too close to Ankergren. The Dane guessed correctly and palmed the ball away as the Leeds contingent massed behind his goal erupted into exultant celebration.

It was the nineteenth minute before Leeds had any possession worthy of the name, but they began to spring some moves of their own. They had weathered Tottenham's initial storm and appeared likely to reach the interval on level terms, but suddenly the home side broke the deadlock.

Bale teased Howson on the left before dipping his shoulder and rounding him to cut the ball back to the edge of the area. Kranjcar fired in a shot which the off-balance Ankergren could only get his foot to. As the ball came out, Crouch poked it low into the corner of the net. You could sense the relief all round White Hart Lane.

The goal did not deter Leeds and combination work from Crowe and Snodgrass down the right earned United a throw deep in Spurs territory after fifty-two minutes. The Scot managed to hold up play and draw a corner out of his markers. Bromby flicked the near post cross goalwards, where it bounced free off Jenas. Beckford reacted instantly, diving to scoop the loose ball over the line for an unexpected equaliser.

Redknapp had seen enough – he brought Palacios off the bench for Rose in an attempt to stiffen the Tottenham midfield. But Leeds now seemed to be the equals of Spurs and were brimming over with confidence. Their passing was assured and accurate across midfield and Beckford was worrying Tottenham defenders with his pace.

After seventy minutes, Redknapp acted again, summoning Roman Pavlyuchenko and Robbie Keane to replace Crouch and Kranjcar in an attempt to finish Leeds off.

Within five minutes, the changes told. An incisive Tottenham move between Palacios and Bale saw a chance set up for Pavlyuchenko. The Russian international calmly stepped over the cross, allowing it to run on to Defoe, sprinted on behind Kisnorbo to reach the perfect return pass and swept coolly into the corner of the net. A masterly goal and one which Spurs were convinced would take them through to the fifth round.

Yet Leeds were still in the tie and Simon Grayson made his own substitution with nine minutes left, sending Becchio on for Doyle.

It looked a forlorn hope as Tottenham continued to knock at the Leeds door. After eighty-one minutes Keane nodded the ball past Ankergren but his effort was disallowed for offside.

Four minutes into stoppage time Beckford claimed a penalty when Dawson tackled him as he ran onto a through ball, but the appeals were ignored. There was a different outcome a minute later, after Howson's long ball was controlled by Beckford in the corner of the Tottenham box. He faced up to Dawson and swerved outside him, drawing a challenge which sent him crashing to the turf. The referee pointed to the spot, much to Dawson's disgust. There were twenty-six seconds of injury-time left.

Beckford, who had missed several important penalties for Leeds over the previous couple of years, strode up to the penalty spot himself, in front of the United fans. There was no doubt this time as Beckford hammered the ball into the roof of the net, utterly beating Gomes' dive and sending the Leeds fans into ecstasy.

Seconds later the final whistle brought the action to an end and Leeds fans danced off into the London night. Grayson was keeping his players' feet on the ground. 'Swindon on Tuesday night,' he reminded them.

He should have saved his breath. The Wiltshire side was on a decent run with a single defeat in ten games, and Leeds just couldn't handle them, slumping to a 3-0 defeat.

United ended their poor run with a sound victory five days later against Colchester courtesy of two Beckford goals.

The Cup exploits ended when Spurs hammered Leeds 3-1 at Elland Road and in truth they were never at the races. Their stuttering form continued and four successive defeats in March seemed to have ended hopes of automatic promotion. Swindon's 3-0 victory at Elland Road on Easter Saturday saw the teams swap places as United ended the day fourth with Norwich skating away at the top and Millwall in second spot.

Grayson was beside himself with frustration but Leeds finally relocated some form with two goals from Naylor at Yeovil on the Monday delivering just the fourth league victory of 2010.

Leeds built on the result, beating Southend and winning at Carlisle.

Swindon had been held at home the previous evening by Exeter and with leaders Norwich losing at Leyton Orient and Millwall drawing at Yeovil, it was a perfect day for United. They climbed into second place, cutting the Canaries' lead to six points and edging away from the chasing pack.

When Millwall lost at Huddersfield on the Friday evening, Leeds were left knowing that three victories out of their final four fixtures would be enough to guarantee promotion. They departed for Gillingham the next day intent on bolstering their chances.

Grayson admitted he was expecting a tough encounter, despite the Gills' lowly position in the table. 'They have a good home record and we know what to expect ... It won't be easy, but it's a game we are capable of winning.'

The match was every bit as challenging as Grayson feared and Leeds were 3-0 down within thirty-three minutes and being played off the park.

Thankfully for the 2,241 fans who had made the 180-mile trek from Yorkshire, a lifeline came seconds before the break courtesy of a smart turn and finish from Becchio.

Ten minutes into the second half, Grayson threw Beckford into the fray and switched to an attack-minded 3-4-3 formation. Leeds continued to dominate both territory and possession but Gillingham goalkeeper Alan Julian was rarely called into action. Instead, a succession of increasingly ambitious shots from distance sailed wide of the target as United huffed and puffed. They pulled a second goal back five minutes from time courtesy of Beckford after he was bundled to the floor by Bentley inside the penalty area and Alan Wiley pointed to the spot. They could not find an equaliser and took the journey home in downbeat mood.

Charlton lost at home to already promoted Norwich, while Swindon were held at the County Ground by Walsall, so no lasting damage was done. Leeds remained in second place, still in charge of their own destiny. In the circumstances, however, the home game with MK Dons on 24 April assumed 'must win' status.

Beckford was left on the bench with Becchio and Gradel up front. They both scored and Beckford came on to add a brace in the final ten minutes to top off an emphatic 4-1 victory against a side that had three men dismissed.

The victory ensured United remained second in the table on eighty-three points, with Millwall's defeat of Leyton Orient keeping them a point behind.

The Elland Road goal fest had restored parity between the two teams' goal difference, a matter that could yet prove decisive. Charlton and Swindon both drew and with two games remaining, the final promotion place seemed to rest between Leeds and Millwall.

Both sides lost on 1 May, with Tranmere seeing off the South Londoners. Knowing that Millwall were two-down, Grayson went for broke at Charlton, throwing on three strikers with the sides level. Naylor's own goal two minutes from time gifted the points to the Addicks.

The draw would have been no use to Leeds other than to end Charlton's chance of catching them. The Whites would still need to beat Bristol Rovers at Elland Road in their final game. Charlton, Millwall, Huddersfield and Swindon were all in with a chance of pipping Leeds to the one remaining automatic promotion spot.

The manager rang the changes. Richard Naylor was out injured and a weary Rob Snodgrass was named among the subs. Leigh Bromby was recalled to the centre of defence and Jermaine Beckford started for the first time in a month. He was also appointed captain for a game that was rumoured to be his farewell appearance before a free transfer to Everton.

It was an extraordinary day, full of high drama; it even had the obligatory pantomime villain for the supporters to boo to their hearts' content.

There was a season's best 38,000 crowd packed into a stadium that buzzed with electricity, albeit tinged with anxiety.

After three minutes, the news came in of the first score of import: Daniel Ward slammed home a low volley for fourth-placed Swindon at Millwall after a free kick from former Leeds midfielder Jonathan Douglas. It took the Wiltshire side (85 points) above Leeds (84). With Huddersfield (83) going ahead seconds earlier at Exeter, Millwall (82) were down to fifth.

At 3.15, there was more drama involving Douglas at Millwall, when he brought down Shaun Batt in the area. Steve Morison made no mistake with the penalty for the South Londoners to make it 1-1; United were back up to second with the Lions restored to third.

Nine minutes later, Nicky Bailey put Charlton ahead at Oldham to draw the Addicks level on eighty-four points with Leeds. Huddersfield conceded at Exeter, dropping them back to sixth.

As fortunes fluctuated wildly, the Whites continued to push on in the feverish atmosphere of Elland Road. The jumpiness of the players mirrored the agitation of the crowd. As chance after chance went begging, nerves took hold. In the stands, unease gave way to unrest.

When Beckford managed to put the ball into the Rovers' net after thirty-two minutes, he saw his effort ruled out for offside by referee Graham Salisbury. And then the game boiled over with an ugly confrontation that might have destroyed United's season.

A coming together between Max Gradel and Daniel Jones left the winger writhing on the floor. He went looking to right the wrong he felt he had suffered and took the law into his own hands, stamping on Jones. The Rovers player threw himself to the turf, theatrically clutching his face as the diminutive Gradel towered righteously over him.

There was a mass confrontation between the teams and angry pushing and shoving.

After consulting his assistant, referee Salisbury sent Gradel from the field. The Leeds player was a man possessed, pointing at the mark of studs on his socks. He reacted furiously, impulsively seeking to confront both Salisbury and Jones.

It required the determined intervention of Beckford and Doyle to persuade Gradel to leave the playing arena. Indeed, Doyle had to physically hoist Gradel off the field when he would not respond to the pushing and shoving of Beckford. Gradel wasn't finished and returned for another go. Two hefty stewards led him down the tunnel as Grayson sought to reorganise the ten men who remained.

Jones was cautioned for his part in proceedings and roundly booed thereafter, while Salisbury was heckled with taunts of 'This game's too big for you', as the siege mentality at Elland Road boiled over.

United's afternoon worsened two minutes after the interval as Bristol took a shock lead. Villain of the peace Jones made space outside Hughes before looping a centre beyond the far post. Leeds had enough defenders in attendance to feel comfortable but they assumed the cross was sailing out for a goal kick. Kuffour was there to hook it back across the face of goal and Duffy was given time to get the ball under control before firing past goalkeeper Shane Higgs. It was one of only two on-target Rovers efforts all afternoon.

Almost simultaneously, Charlton took a 2-0 lead at Oldham. The way the results stood, Charlton (84 points) were in second, followed by Leeds, Millwall and Swindon (all on 83) as the tension reached boiling point.

Grayson threw caution to the wind and brought Howson on for Lowry. Within five minutes, the Leeds-born midfielder sent the crowd into raptures with an equaliser struck as sweetly as could be imagined.

Howson had already had three sighters on goal when Johnson's miscued long ball from the left found Becchio on the edge of the area. He laid it back for Howson who curled it home beautifully. The home fans exploded with relief as the young schemer demanded their vocal support.

Three minutes later, the news came through that Millwall (85 points) had leapfrogged Leeds and Charlton (both 84) by taking a 2-1 lead against Swindon (82).

But the momentum was with Leeds and the fervent crowd went wild when their heroes took the lead after sixty-three minutes.

Goalkeeper Anderson recklessly attempted to throw the ball quickly to the right flank but his distribution was wild and the ball fell to Johnson on the left. His shot was blocked but the ball sat up nicely and goalscorer supreme Beckford was on it in a flash to scuff a shot under the keeper and over the line for his thirty-first goal of the season.

Cue Bedlam at Elland Road as United regained second place in the table ...

With one goal between the teams and tension gnawing hungrily away, this was to be no cakewalk.

United pushed anxiously for the third goal that would make the game safe but were thankful to Higgs when the keeper dived bravely to gather at the feet of Kuffour. It was every bit as vital a contribution as the goals of Howson and Beckford.

Leeds won a free kick on the right when Lines climbed all over Becchio. Kilkenny's dead ball to the far post was met powerfully by Bromby, but he headed against the foot of the upright and the ball was cleared.

Over in South London, Millwall kept the pressure on, with Morison putting them 3-1 ahead with a spectacular strike from distance. Billy Paynter glanced home a header from Alan Sheehan's free kick to bring Swindon back to 3-2, but as long as Leeds retained their lead they would be up.

With the game edging into five minutes of injury-time, the manager sent Snodgrass on for Beckford, who went off to a hero's farewell, pausing to symbolically hand the captain's armband to Howson.

With the tension almost too much to bear, referee Salisbury blew his whistle to signify the end of the game. The contest was finally over and Leeds had held out for a memorable victory.

All the official requests to stay off the pitch were ignored. The massive crowd were not going to let a moment like this pass quietly after so many years of frustration. Thousands poured onto the playing surface in ecstatic celebration. It took a plea from Simon Grayson to restore some order so the players could come out for a well-deserved lap of honour and join in the fun.

Grayson described the win as a 'fantastic achievement. We didn't do it the easy way after going down to ten men and a goal behind early in the second half. Credit to the players. It was a fantastic effort from everybody ... It's never easy when you've got ten men to play with, but we've got belief and determination that we could do it. They kept going right until the end. Full credit to them. They are a fantastic bunch of players to work with.'

CHAPTER FOURTEEN
Missing the Boat

You can spend years chasing something and then you finally get it – it's a strange feeling, like, 'So what was that all about?' It also means you have to start thinking about the next steps, the next goal.

That's what it was like for Leeds United Football Club in the summer of 2010. Promotion from League One achieved, Simon Grayson and Ken Bates had to work out how to maintain their new-found status. The preceding three years would have been wasted if the club were to go straight back down. Much as it pained Bates, he would have to open his wallet and fund the development of the squad. He'd already had to fork out for significant promotion bonuses and now he had to find the money to give Grayson a fighting chance. There was a profit for the season of £2.1 million to fall back on and the promise of a £5 million increase in television money reduced the degree of any sympathy. United fans demanded that he splashed the cash.

At the same time, Bates was determined to continue with his plans to develop the Elland Road stadium and work was completed on the Centenary Pavilion. Much of his ambition was geared towards England's bid to host the 2018 World Cup finals with Elland Road one of the venues scheduled for use. The failure of the bid was a key setback. Bates still had the option to buy the ground from Teak Commercial for £14.5 million, which would have made an awful lot of sense as it was valued at £49 million, but with the end of World Cup hopes went his urgency. Bates simply wasn't prepared to finance the deal in the circumstances, despite numerous promises to the fans.

He knew that if Leeds were to gain promotion to the Premiership, then he would have a bill of £4.8 million as a condition of his 2007 buyout and a further £1.5m in windfall payments on transfers. The money washing about in the Premiership would have made that a decent trade-off, but big buys to get there were too much of a gamble for Bates. The club's accounts muttered darkly that 'the board will continue their strategic investment in the playing squad be that by way of transfer fee or increased salary payments to Bosman-type signings.'

There was one marquee signing, goalkeeper Kasper Schmeichel, son of Manchester United legend Peter, but the deal didn't cost Bates a penny. Notts County and Schmeichel agreed to cancel his contract by mutual consent in order to get the player off the wage bill as the Meadow Lane club's own big spending plans collapsed.

It was rumoured that Schmeichel never received any wages while he was at County. He had been so desperate for first-team football after eight appearances in four years at Manchester City that he was prepared to tolerate it for a while, but his patience was exhausted.

Schmeichel's wage was eye-watering but Bates managed to hold salary inflation as a whole down to £2.8 million (20 per cent), some achievement in a division where the payroll for many clubs exceeded their turnover.

A host of potential signings were mooted without coming to fruition, including Sheffield United midfielder Nick Montgomery, Watford's John Eustace, former left-back Ian Harte, Arsenal keeper Wojciech Szczesny, former striker Rob Hulse, Doncaster poacher Billy Sharp and Hamilton midfielder James McArthur.

Grayson himself signed a new three-year contract during the summer despite what Bates called 'enticing offers' from rival clubs, including Leicester City.

In terms of transfers, Grayson insisted that he had to get players who wanted 'to come for the right reasons. I think we're always going to be linked with players because of the club we are ... It's not about getting loads of money, it's about playing for a top club ... We're working hard on a lot of things to get a few in because we want to have a better squad capable of doing well in the Championship.'

In addition to Schmeichel, the club brought in Swindon front man Billy Paynter, Derby right-back Paul Connolly, Swansea left-back Federico Bessone, Charlton wide man Lloyd Sam, Ipswich centre-back Alex Bruce and Cardiff forward Ross McCormack.

They had big shoes to fill with United talisman Jermaine Beckford leaving at the end of his contract for Premiership Everton.

There were other departures, with United declining to renew the contracts of Casper Ankergren, Rui Marques, Tresor Kandol and Alan Sheehan.

Grayson commented, 'It is the hardest part of a manager's job, informing players who have contributed to a successful season that you are not going to offer them a new contract ... The club needs to move forward and these decisions, as hard as they were, had to be made in that interest.'

The first day brought a disappointing defeat at home to Derby, but Leeds quickly adjusted to life in the Championship and had edged into the play-off zone by the end of August, impressing many critics with their football.

With Paynter sidelined by a shin injury sustained in pre-season, Grayson was forced to adopt a 4-3-2-1 formation with Gradel and Snodgrass flanking Becchio as lone spearhead. It had been expected that he would go 4-4-2 with Paynter and Becchio operating in harness. The change appeared to benefit Leeds' football and they certainly settled well to their work, demonstrating that they were able to more than hold their own in the higher division.

For a while, South African striker Davide Somma looked like he would be the man to replace Beckford after bursting to prominence on his league debut with two late goals against Millwall. 'Like Jermaine, I'd always back myself to take a high proportion of the chances that come my way,' said Somma. 'I am confident of my ability to score twenty goals a season at this level.'

In the end, however, it was Becchio who became the key striker.

Momentum was stayed by a 5-2 defeat at Barnsley on 14 September and there was an even more extraordinary reverse two weeks later at home to Preston.

Leeds conceded early but were 4-1 ahead six minutes before the end of the first half. Two of the goals came from Somma.

On this particular night, the headlines were stolen by North End's Jon Parkin, whose hat-trick inspired his side to a comeback of epic proportions. They pulled a second goal back before the break and then ran in four goals without reply to deliver a remarkable 6-4 victory.

A raging Grayson labelled the result as 'embarrassing', adding, 'Football never surprises you; you are going well and suddenly it kicks you where it hurts again. I still had a go at the players at half-time, because we had given them far too many opportunities. When we were 4-1 up, we needed to be more professional, but we gave them a chance to get back into the game. There were far too many errors – both individually and collectively. We made stupid mistakes and it cost us. To lose 6-4 at home is unbelievable.'

The following day, Grayson dragged the players into Thorp Arch to dissect video footage of the horror show.

The team took a while to get the shock out of their system, but after losing 4-0 at home to Cardiff on 25 October they launched an eight-game unbeaten run which carried them up to fourth.

On 18 December, Elland Road played host to pace setters QPR. An early morning clean-up operation was launched to ensure the pitch was playable after overnight snow in Leeds and temperatures falling to six below.

Grayson's side played with confidence and verve. With Max Gradel enjoying his best game in a Leeds shirt, they demonstrated a finishing edge that hinted at hopes of automatic promotion.

3 May 2014 – Brian McDermott acknowledges supporters after the home draw with Derby. He was gone before the start of the following season, the first victim of 'Manager Eater' Massimo Cellino. (Copyright Heidi Haigh)

19 July 2014 – David Hockaday poses with a fan during pre-season at Guiseley. (Copyright Heidi Haigh)

11 November 2014 – Adryan and Mirco Antenucci help Souleymane Doukara celebrate his goal in the victory over Blackpool. The trio were part of an influx of foreign signings at the start of the 2014/15 season. (Copyright Heidi Haigh)

25 April 2015 – Neil Redfearn oversees the victory at Sheffield Wednesday. Liam Cooper is in the foreground. (Copyright Heidi Haigh)

30 January 2016 – Massimo Cellino looks on as Leeds win at Bolton in the FA Cup. (Copyright Heidi Haigh)

15 February 2016 – Fans show their opposition to Cellino with a light show before the game against Middlesbrough. (Copyright Heidi Haigh)

19 March 2016 – Time to Go Massimo! Hours later Leeds lost 4-1 at home to Huddersfield. (Copyright Heidi Haigh)

12 April 2016 – Stuart Dallas celebrates as his two goals secure victory at Birmingham. Lewis Cook, Charlie Taylor, Chris Wood and Mirco Antenucci lend their support. (Copyright Heidi Haigh)

16 May 2016 – Steve Evans watches as Leeds end their season with a draw at Preston. Former Leeds boss Simon Grayson leads the opposition. Weeks later, Evans was sacked. (Copyright Heidi Haigh)

22 July 2016 – Garry Monk answers questions during pre-season at Guiseley. (Copyright Heidi Haigh)

17 September 2016 – Chris Wood celebrates his penalty at Cardiff. The New Zealand international enjoyed a memorable season. (Copyright Heidi Haigh)

29 October 2016 – Pontus Jansson after victory against Burton. The big Swede formed a massive bond with the fans with some wholehearted displays. (Copyright Heidi Haigh)

17 April 2017 – Rob Green prepares to face Wolves at Elland Road. He couldn't prevent a 1-0 defeat. (Copyright Heidi Haigh)

6 August 2017 – Thomas Christiansen is tense as he watches the opening-day victory at Bolton. (Copyright Heidi Haigh)

25 August 2018 – Mateusz Klich gets all the congratulations after opening the scoring at Norwich. Pontus Jansson, Kemar Roofe, Ezgjan Alioski, Kalvin Phillips and Luke Ayling get in on the act. (Copyright Heidi Haigh)

16 March 2019 – Pontus Jansson takes over in goal after Kiko Casilla's dismissal against Sheffield United. The defeat unhinged Leeds' season. (Copyright Heidi Haigh)

20 April 2019 – Pablo Hernandez blows a penalty chance against Wigan on a drab day for Leeds. (Copyright Heidi Haigh)

15 May 2019 – Pontus Jansson consoles Pablo Hernandez after play-off failure against Derby. (Copyright Heidi Haigh)

15 May 2019 – Kalvin Phillips seeks solace with Leeds fans after play-off despair against Derby. (Copyright Heidi Haigh)

1 October 2019 – Ben White and West Brom's former Leeds defender Kyle Bartley await a corner. (Copyright Heidi Haigh)

5 October 2019 – Marcelo Bielsa makes a point during the defeat at Millwall. (Copyright Heidi Haigh)

30 November 2019 – Marcelo Bielsa poses with Leeds fan and author Heidi Haigh before the game with Middlesbrough. (Copyright Heidi Haigh)

Right: 30 November 2019 – Mateusz Klich (top right) curls in an exquisite fourth against Middlesbrough. (Copyright Heidi Haigh)

Below: 22 December 2019 – Stuart Dallas (second left) gets the fourth goal in the astonishing 5-4 victory at Birmingham. (Copyright Heidi Haigh)

1 February 2020 – Pablo Hernandez (far left) about to fire in a free kick against Wigan. The home defeat nearly derailed Leeds. (Copyright Dave Tomlinson)

August 2020 – The statue of Don Revie overlooks Elland Road. (Copyright Dave Tomlinson)

August 2020 – *Marching on Together* mural at the entrance to the subway leading to the stadium, featuring Gary Speed, David Batty, Howard Wilkinson, Gary McAllister and Gordon Strachan. (Copyright Dave Tomlinson)

September 2020 – Elland Road, home of the Gods. (Copyright Dave Tomlinson)

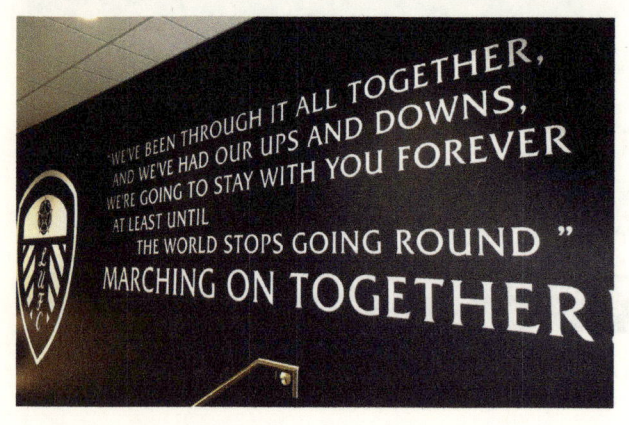

December 2017 – Marching on Together! (Copyright Heidi Haigh)

Leeds looked dangerous from the start, Becchio's header from Connolly's cross drawing a flying save from goalkeeper Paddy Kenny. The impressive Snodgrass also went close with a drive.

Nevertheless, when Leeds went ahead it was against the run of play. Howson met Snodgrass' hopeful cross to the back post and as the ball looped up Gradel reacted swiftest to half-volley the ball over the line.

The West Londoners began the second half looking the stronger of the two teams but after a period of Rangers pressure, Gradel picked up Collins' clearance well inside his own half, ran uninterrupted into the QPR area and turned Fitz Hall inside out before firing the ball between goalkeeper Paddy Kenny and his near post.

It was United's most comprehensive performance of the season, overshadowing even Howson-inspired victories at Scunthorpe and Burnley and Becchio's hat-trick against Bristol City.

The day ended perfectly with the club announcing that Becchio had signed a new three-and-a-half-year contract.

'I said when I came back that someone would take this club back to the Premier League,' smiled Grayson. 'No one knows when that will be but there is an expectancy level and, hopefully, we can achieve it in the not-too-distant future. The League position will only be significant at the end of the season when you can't win any more games … We have a lot of hard games coming up in a short space of time. It is a tight division.

'Some of our attacking play was a real testament as to what these players can do. We have to try and build on what was a really big performance. I thought we saw the game out really well and showed a lot of football knowledge. The way we kept possession in the last five to ten minutes was pleasing. You can sense the players are enjoying what they are doing at the moment.'

Grayson seemed to have hit upon the right combination going forward with Kilkenny and Johnson providing a sound platform in midfield, Howson given a roving role and Snodgrass and Gradel providing ammunition for Becchio down the middle. The Argentine provided a real cutting edge, enjoying a wonderful season in front of goal.

Three successive draws and defeat at Cardiff halted the momentum as Grayson prepared his charges for a big money FA Cup tie at Arsenal.

Leeds rose to the occasion admirably, taking the lead by way of a second-half penalty from Snodgrass. They looked set to spring a major surprise until substitute Cesc Fabregas equalised from the penalty spot after ninety minutes to rescue Arsenal.

The Gunners righted the wrongs in the Elland Road replay, winning 3-1, though Leeds had the goal of the night with Johnson's stunning drive from distance.

Championship Manager of the Month Grayson enthused over Leeds' performance over the two games, though he admitted Arsenal had been the best side on the night. 'The players can be proud of what they achieved with their work ethic, the way they passed it at times, and an attitude to never give in.'

Grayson's attention was firmly on promotion and he knew that Leeds had to strengthen to add weight to their challenge. Things looked promising when Ken Bates assured him that the Cup windfall would be made available for transfers.

Bates heaped praise on Grayson. 'With all the madness in football, he's probably one of the longest-serving managers in the league. He's brought stability to the club and he's not a headline seeker. He's just got on with his job. We've supported him in every way we can and in every way we can afford. But in saying that, his demands are not excessive and he's realistic. He's respected by everyone and he's got a cool head. When we lose, I don't get panic calls the next morning saying, "we've got to do this, that or the other." There's just a cold assessment of what went wrong and how we can put it right. I've got great hopes for Simon and I hope he's here for many years to come.'

There were plenty of rumours about incoming transfers, including shock moves for former stars Alan Smith and Jonathan Woodgate but the January window ended with only two deals. Grayson extended Sunderland left-back George McCartney's loan deal and completed the permanent transfer of Bolton centre-back Andy O'Brien.

Both men had shown impressive form during United's unbeaten run, but supporters seethed with indignation that all Bates' promises of investment came to nothing.

Grayson dutifully trotted out the party line that he had never intended to spend big and wouldn't sign players just for the sake of it, but he recognised that it was a missed opportunity. He was left to scrabble around in the loan market, bringing in American full-back Eric Lichaj and midfielders Barry Bannan and Jake Livermore, but they struggled to make an impact as United's promotion charge faltered.

There were some decent one-off results – a 5-2 defeat of Doncaster and Billy Paynter finally opening his scoring account when he netted the winner at Preston. A 4-1 hammering of rivals Nottingham Forest on 2 April seemed to have secured United's participation in the play-offs but subsequent defeats at Millwall and Derby and home draws with Watford and Reading saw them slip out of the top six for the first time since November.

The hamstring injury that saw Becchio limp out of the Watford game ended his season and deprived Leeds of their greatest goal threat, a man with twenty goals to his credit.

The death knell came on Easter Monday as Leeds lost at relegation-threatened Crystal Palace, though Grayson refused to admit defeat until the fat lady was trilling.

A 1-0 defeat at Selhurst Park left Leeds three points behind sixth-placed Forest with two games to play, but Grayson insisted, 'Until it's impossible, we'll keep going.'

The home game with eighth-placed Burnley was crucial and Grayson gave Ross McCormack just his fifth Championship start of the season. The Scot repaid him with the only goal of the game and showed what the fans had been missing all season.

'He's had to be patient,' said Grayson. 'When I bought him in the summer, he would have thought he'd be one of the two strikers we would play in a 4-4-2, but he got injured, we changed the system and his opportunities have been few and far between. But testament to the lad. He's kept working hard in training, he's looked really sharp over the last few weeks and that's why we played him today. His movement we thought would cause Burnley problems and it did and the bonus was he got his goal as well.'

The points took Leeds past Burnley and Millwall, but they remained three points behind Forest and with a goal difference inferiority of six.

To all intents and purposes, United's challenge was done but in the final game McCormack snatched the winning goal against champions QPR to give hints of both what might have been and what 2011/12 could bring.

There were positive noises from both Grayson and Bates about summer strengthening to support a real promotion push, but Bates' promise of cash to spend once more came to nothing. The heart was ripped out of Grayson's team with Schmeichel, Johnson, Kilkenny and Gradel leaving after refusing to accept contract offers, protesting at Bates' parsimony.

The chairman formalised his ownership of the club with a supposed buyout by his company, Outro Limited. Bates' critics thought it was an artifice to put to rest protests about the opaque nature of United's ownership. Certainly, it followed surprisingly quickly after questions about the club's ownership were raised during a Select Committee inquiry into football.

If the move smacked of cynicism there was a distinct feeling of unease at the arrival of limited newcomers like Michael Brown, Andy Lonergan and Darren O'Dea. United were undoubtedly weakened although the arrival on a loan-to-buy deal of Wolves striker Andy Keogh, who had started his career at Elland Road, was welcomed as a positive move. He hinted at having 'unfinished business' and certainly performed well early season, but there was no lasting improvement in results.

Frustrated supporters bristled with indignation at plans for a multi-million development of the East Stand and urged Bates to 'Build us a team, not a hotel'. The accounts revealed that £5 million from season ticket sales for 2012/13 and 2013/14 had been committed to a scheme with an estimated cost of £7 million. These funds were supplemented by the issue of £3.1 million in preference shares which were guaranteed to pay out £4 million when redeemed, netting Bates' Lutonville Holdings a tax-free profit of £1 million. The company banked a six-figure sum in the meantime, including £100,000 as a set-up fee and £40,000 each quarter for 'monitoring fees'. Lutonville loaned the club a further million in March 2012.

There was a mood of bitter resentment among supporters as it became apparent that Bates was looking to take the money and run, though he talked bullishly of 'fully backing Simon financially'.

The sad truth was that Leeds were nowhere near. There was an emotional 4-0 victory at Forest as Leeds supporters offered a tribute to former player Gary Speed, who had committed suicide. United showed what they could really do, with midfielders Howson and Clayton outstanding and Snodgrass a real threat out wide.

More typical of Leeds' form was the 5-0 defeat at home to Blackpool that spelled the end at Elland Road for keeper Paul Rachubka and the sight of lowly Barnsley doing the double over their Yorkshire rivals. Leeds were tenth after three defeats in a row in the second half of December, with promotion hopes slipping away.

Grayson continued to insist that his men could still win promotion, but his words were ringing hollow. He faced speculation about his future on New Year's Eve when United crashed 4-1 at Barnsley and he rounded on the players after a fourth game without a win. It was by some way the worst performance in that spell.

Bates had been hounded for months by *Guardian* investigative journalist David Conn and campaigning MPs and a critical BBC documentary, *Who Owns Leeds United?* pushed him to the limit. He lashed out, banning both *The Guardian* and the BBC from Elland Road, and slated the fans who protested against his stinginess, labelling them 'Morons'. His strategy was to deflect any criticism onto Grayson.

After seemingly commending United's standing in the table, Bates added, 'You also have got to do soul-searching on why we have lost the games we've lost and why have we drawn the games we've drawn. And, without being too critical, the fact of the matter is we have lost games rather than be beaten. We have given away the points rather than them being earned by the opposition and that's something that we've had too much of and it's got to stop. There are discussions going on this week, heart-searching in the backroom to decide what we can do to improve the situation because we should be higher than we are.'

As he turned eighty, Bates told the *Daily Express*, 'We need to get promoted this year. Not financially but for the fans' sake. I actually spoke to Simon Grayson about it after the Barnsley game. He reassured me that we were going to get promoted, so I said to him, "How come we're fifth then?" We'll see.'

Come December, Bates' sermon had moved on. 'He stands and falls by his results. Obviously, if he does not deliver, he knows his job is on the line and that applies to all managers. Simon and his backroom staff don't have a bad record. This year is the ultimate challenge for him, his staff and, just as importantly, the players.'

After claiming for weeks that the club was moving closer to renewing the contract of Jonny Howson, Bates sold the skipper to Norwich as the end of the January transfer window approached. He claimed that any other course of action would lead to Howson leaving for nothing at the end of the contract and declared the sale as sound business. He insisted the sale was fully supported by Grayson. The supporters bayed their derision, declaring that Leeds were confirmed as a selling club and that Bates lacked ambition.

When United lost 4-1 at home to Birmingham on the last day of the window, Bates swung the axe, dispensing with the services of a man who less than two years earlier had led the club to promotion.

'It came to a head when Simon wanted to sign a midfielder which would have cost the club nearly £1.5 million over the length of his proposed contract,' wrote Bates in his programme notes for the following game against Brighton. 'We already have nine midfield players, so I refused – the first time ever! In the circumstances it was decided to part company with Simon and his staff immediately following the Birmingham result.'

Grayson had suspected his days were numbered but was devastated at being unable to finish the job he had started.

'I got on well with him, but you did feel as well like you're let down because you wanted to move forward,' said Grayson several years later. 'I just don't think the club had the money to do it. And did they have the ambition to do it? Probably not. They'd seen what the club had gone through financially and didn't want to go through that. But the odd little gamble … I wasn't wanting millions on players. Half a million on this, that and the other would have helped us get over the line.'

Grayson had identified two defenders who could have solved problems – QPR defender Kaspars Gorkss and thirty-two-year-old Gareth McAuley, who had six months left on his contract at Ipswich.

'They only wanted three or four hundred grand for him. The board decided we didn't need anybody and McAuley was too old. I felt we were so close and another defender would have certainly made us stronger defensively. I didn't want to get away from winning games and attacking, which had been my philosophy ever since I'd been at Leeds, but I knew we needed to be a little bit tighter with extra quality.'

At the end of the campaign, McAuley left Ipswich to join West Brom in the Premier League, where he spent the next seven years, representing Northern Ireland at Euro 2016.

Rather than strengthen a problem position, Leeds waited until March to sign young midfielders Barry Bannan and Jake Livermore on loan from Aston Villa and Tottenham. If anything, the pair disrupted an area of the side which was working well.

'Of course, it's frustrating because we were that close to getting to where everybody wanted to get to at the first attempt. Who knows if we'd have got promoted that year, but I think [signing a defender] would have given us a better chance of being able to achieve that.

'All of a sudden, this group of players that had done really well for me and are outstanding talents were not getting the contracts they wanted at Leeds.'

Grayson, revealing that Howson had been sold against the wishes of both him and the player, was stung by criticism from Elland Road. He recalled how he used to speak to Bates every day and had been treated like a second son by wife Suzannah. He hadn't heard a thing from the couple since he was sacked. He blamed Bates' right-hand man Gwyn Williams for his dismissal rather than poor results. He fell out badly with Williams, who nurtured the grudge and turned Bates against him.

'I don't regret anything. I worked tirelessly to make it successful. Supporters loved my time there. I loved being with them ... I'm immensely proud of what I achieved and the style of football I brought to the club and how we entertained and the spirit and passion we showed week in, week out. We didn't get everything right, but I'm proud I reconnected the supporters back with the team and the city.'

CHAPTER FIFTEEN
Warnock

'I feel I have one big challenge left in me and believe Leeds is a club that should be in the Premier League,' commented Neil Warnock. 'I want to be the man who is able to deliver this for a set of fans who never cease to amaze me with their numbers and their loyalty. Having met with Ken Bates, it was an easy decision to take up the challenge.'

And so, former Sheffield United, Crystal Palace and QPR manager Warnock introduced himself to the world as the new manager of Leeds United. His management CV contained another nine clubs and he had engineered seven promotions, a record he shared with Dave Bassett, Graham Taylor and Jim Smith. Three of those successes came in the Championship as he led Notts County, Sheffield United and QPR against the odds into the Premiership. Everyone was curious as to whether Warnock could repeat the feat at Leeds, although those welcoming his appointment were in the minority. The larger-than-life manager had rubbed rival supporters up the wrong way the length and breadth of the country and the memory of Leeds fans went back a long way.

Shortly after sacking Simon Grayson, Ken Bates and chief executive Shaun Harvey were pictured deep in conversation with Warnock at the Café de Paris in Monte Carlo's Casino Square, ironing out the details of his contract. The challenge of reviving Leeds was enough to persuade Warnock to reject offers from Wolves and Huddersfield Town, the latter offering a £1 million salary.

Originally, Bates and Warnock had agreed to keep the news under wraps until the Monday following the 18 February game with Doncaster. 'However, on my flight back from Monaco I looked again at the Championship table,' wrote Warnock, 'We had a local derby at home to Doncaster we really had to win. I realised I could not afford to wait, as defeat could have created a nigh on unbridgeable gap between us and the play-off places. I rang the chairman and said I thought I ought to attend the game, and if necessary get involved. He agreed, so we had to announce the appointment.

'I think events proved it was the right decision. We were losing at half-time so I decided it was time to come down from the stand; forty-five minutes later we had three points. Obviously, I'm a tactical genius!'

Doncaster made it 2-0 just minutes after the resumption. 'Fortunately, we soon got one back, and if anything showed me the club's potential it was the reaction from the supporters. Suddenly the stadium was alive with sound; it was magnificent. The fans willed us on to victory. I was punching the air with the rest of them when the injury-time winner went in. It doesn't matter what age you are, a late winning goal is always a thrill. The trick now is maintaining that momentum.'

Doing so proved more difficult than Warnock hoped with goalless draws at Portsmouth and Hull sandwiching a defeat at home to Southampton. A two-goal victory at Middlesbrough raised the spirits and prompted a claim that 'We're not out of the chase yet,' but Leeds had more disappointments at Elland Road, held to a draw by West Ham and then on the wrong end of an extraordinary 7-3 defeat to Forest.

Snodgrass' penalty gave Leeds the lead before Forest opened up a 3-1 lead in the seven minutes after the break. Leeds quickly levelled with goals from Becchio and Brown. They should have had the momentum to push on for a win, but Garath McCleary added three goals to his earlier effort and Dexter Blackstock added his second goal nine minutes from time to top off a remarkable triumph.

It was the first time that Leeds had ever conceded seven times in a league match at Elland Road. 'You learn more about your players at moments like this, rather than when you're winning,' said Warnock. 'It tells you who is prepared to stand up and be counted; who you want alongside you in the trenches.'

Leeds bounced back to win at Millwall, but then lost five of their final seven games to limp into a disappointing fourteenth-place finish, four positions lower than they were when Grayson was sacked.

'There's a sense of relief that it's all over,' sighed Warnock. 'I'm disappointed with the way we lost but I've known for four or five weeks what type of job it was going to be here ... It's bigger than I thought and it might be even bigger again. I don't know yet whether certain lads will re-sign or not.'

Warnock's urgent need to rebuild was stymied – cash was in short supply and Bates had been looking for investment for months. There was at least one genuinely interested party and a confidentiality agreement was agreed with an unnamed bidder which allowed it access to the books.

Leeds United Supporters' Trust (LUST) broke the news at the end of May. United quickly confirmed 'that talks are taking place regarding investment for the long-term future', though details were sketchy. With a seriously interested investor, Bates didn't want anything to go wrong.

He did his best to rubbish LUST, focusing his attention on chairman Gary Cooper. He used his Yorkshire Radio mouthpiece to broadcast two interviews on the matter, including publicising details of Cooper's personal ticket purchasing history, painting him as a rare attendee at matches and therefore not authorised to speak for 'the ordinary Leeds United fan'. In April, broadcasting watchdog Ofcom upheld Cooper's complaint of 'unfair and unjust treatment and unwarranted infringement of privacy'.

Speculation continued to proliferate with Bates rumoured to have priced the club at £80 million while 'a mystery Canadian consortium' had offered £40 million. Others talked about an interested party from the United States, and it became apparent that there were multiple bidders. At the end of June, the club confirmed that an exclusivity period had been agreed with an unidentified party to allow it to complete due diligence. It added that the prospective investor had 'the financial resources to support the club' and expressed confidence that they would pass the Football League's Fit and Proper Persons Test, an assessment of the suitability of major shareholders.

Warnock's transfer dealings were complicated by the intrigue and, while it was said that the buyout would provide long-term wherewithal, United did not have the funds to secure his targets. Worse still, club captain Rob Snodgrass was prevaricating over signing a new deal because of the uncertainty and potential suitors were circling.

Eventually, Snodgrass threw his lot in with Norwich City, following the example of former teammates Bradley Johnson and Jonny Howson, causing further unrest among supporters.

Eventually, Warnock managed to scrape together enough money to get things moving and brought in a number of new men, including Jason Pearce, Paddy Kenny, Lee Peltier, Luke Varney, David Norris, Michael Tonge, Paul Green, Rudy Austin and El-Hadji Diouf.

They were typical Warnock signings, and the supporters sighed with dismay.

On the opening day of the season, Warnock handed out nine debuts against Wolves. One of them was eighteen-year-old Sam Byram, brought in from the Academy to cover the problem right-back position. Byram had an outstanding debut and Leeds began with a win thanks to a goal from Becchio. All the attention, however, was on the directors' box where Bates was accompanied by representatives from the potential buyers, soon to be revealed as GFH Capital, a Dubai-based investment company and bank.

There were rumours that the buyout was 'imminent', but negotiations dragged on and on. It was Christmas before the deal was completed.

Amidst all the distractions and rumour mongering, Leeds' form was patchy and their performances uninspiring. They plunged towards the relegation zone after a dispiriting 6-1 defeat at home to Watford on 10 November. Leeds ended the game with nine men after Pearce was dismissed and Austin stretchered off with a suspected broken leg. Warnock's comment that 'I can't fault the lads' didn't go down well with the supporters. Over the months they had witnessed some dreadful play. Warnock's predilection for 'Hoofball' had driven the hope out of them.

All the time, Warnock assured them that things would improve in the near future when there was money to spend in the transfer window. 'Then you'll see a real Neil Warnock side.'

More positively, Warnock showed his true colours when he steered Leeds through an exciting assault on the Capital One Cup. Shrewsbury and Oxford were mundane opponents, but then Leeds took Premier League scalps in the shape of Everton and Southampton. The Everton game in particular was a good old-fashioned giant killing as Leeds blew their illustrious opponents away on a rainswept evening at Elland Road. As the GFH Capital takeover neared its final act, the run ended with a 5-1 defeat to Chelsea at Elland Road. Another shock had been on the cards when Becchio opened the scoring, but the Londoners found their feet and their goalscoring touch to hammer Leeds.

GFH Capital's takeover was duly completed on 21 December when they acquired 100 per cent of the share capital. Deputy chief executive David Haigh, company director Salem Patel and Gulf Finance House interim chief executive Hisham Al Rayes were appointed to the board and a bright future was forecast for Leeds United Football Club.

CHAPTER SIXTEEN
GFH Capital

'We're looking forward to a bright future,' said David Haigh as GFH gave their first press conference as owners of Leeds United. 'This is a fresh start for the football club and we welcome fans both old and new to Elland Road. We've had over 4,000 emails of support from fans and we've been overwhelmed by the reaction. Everyone we've spoken to in the city has been fantastic and the atmosphere [against Chelsea] was incredible. We look forward to bringing more of the same to Elland Road.'

Haigh shamelessly appealed to the fans' desire for the return of United's glory glory days. He was pictured with GFH colleague Salem Patel, bedecked in blue, gold and white scarves, in obligatory publicity photos at Elland Road bearing wide grins and huge promises.

The takeover was widely welcomed, although the fans were enraged by the revelation that Ken Bates would remain as chairman until the end of the season when he would revert to president. So much for a brave new future ...

There was massive disillusionment when the much-anticipated investment in the transfer window did not materialise, despite Hisham Al Rayes' promise that a separate budget had been set aside to support United's promotion ambitions. GFH found the money in November to bring in wide man Jerome Thomas and centre-back Alan Tate on loan, with the promise that their deals would become substantive, but even those hopes evaporated.

The initial signs were good with the two newcomers prompting victory against Palace and a three-game winning run which climaxed with a stunning 4-2 victory at Huddersfield, but Leeds failed to kick on.

If anything, Leeds were diminished in the transfer window, with top scorer Becchio adding to the growing numbers of former Leeds players at Norwich. Steve Morison made the reverse journey with £200,000 thrown in as a perfunctory bonus. Aston Villa left-back Stephen Warnock arrived on a free transfer and the obscure African striker Habib Habibou signed a short-lived loan deal that offered little. It was too depressing for words.

There was little to write home about other than an FA Cup victory against Premiership Tottenham courtesy of goals from Luke Varney and Ross McCormack. The fans began venting their spleen, infuriated by the poor football and excuse-laden press conferences.

The enthusiasm that greeted GFH's interest in the club had rapidly degenerated into a world-weary resignation as the fans poured out their anger, insisting loudly to Neil Warnock that it was 'Time to go' and advising GFH that 'You don't know what you're doing'.

Leeds had been in a tantalising eighth spot at Christmas, but any hope of promotion evaporated as they stumbled through a series of nondescript draws and depressing defeats. It was the nature of the football, however, which was the biggest concern, devoid of both passion and intelligence.

And still Warnock mumbled his inane clichés. 'The takeover has given everyone a massive lift ... There will be no one going from here unless we agree to it ... There has been a feel-good factor at the club for a few weeks now ... I know I will get the support ... I thought we worked our socks off ... I think I'm doing a great job if I'm honest ... I spoke to the new owners before the game, we're all pulling in the right direction ... It needed someone with my experience to steady the waters here. I don't know how a younger manager would have coped with everything ... We are bound to be in and around the mix come the end of the season ... I am ever so pleased the way we have played ... I have the team that I want together at the moment. I can't fault anyone now.'

You could hear the bored yawn from the stands, fans struggling even to put the effort into voicing their anger.

Eventually, even Warnock grew tired of his excuses and threw in the towel.

'If we don't go up, I won't be there,' said Warnock on several occasions. 'I think the fans have known it all along and we are eight points off the play-offs now, so it isn't rocket science. I think the club will be sensible about it and I don't want to leave them in the lurch because I think it is a great club and I think in the next couple of years, they will be back in the big time.'

The defeat at home to Derby on 1 April was Leeds' sixth consecutive game without a win and GFH took Warnock at his word, ending his time in the hot seat.

Academy coach Neil Redfearn was asked to take charge while GFH Capital cast their net for a replacement. They missed out on their first choice, Nigel Adkins, but within a fortnight had appointed former Reading manager Brian McDermott in a move that was universally welcomed.

For his part, McDermott was delighted to sign a three-year contract. 'It is entirely possible I wouldn't have taken another job at this stage of the season anywhere else but here,' he admitted, 'This is a massive club with a real history to it, and they are getting a manager and assistant, in Nigel Gibbs, who are very hungry to succeed and, yes, to prove a point.

'There is nothing wrong with that, and I have told the players they have a point to prove as well. They need to step out in this fantastic stadium and show they have got what it takes to feed off the unbelievable atmosphere these fans generate.'

Leeds had the comfort of a five-point cushion over the relegation zone with five games remaining, but it was important that McDermott could hit the ground running. Such a slender advantage could have been easily lost if the players failed to settle quickly.

Happily, there was an instant new manager bounce with two Varney goals seeing off Sheffield Wednesday and Austin scoring the only goal of the game against Burnley. They weren't absolutely safe but were as good as there. As Burnley manager Sean Dyche observed, 'That group of players weren't playing like that two weeks ago. I know because I saw them.'

Joyous supporters sang, 'We're Leeds United, we're passing the ball,' blissfully consigning the memory of Warnock to history.

McDermott glowed with pleasure. 'I've come here to enjoy myself, the staff want to enjoy themselves and I want the players and the fans to enjoy themselves, that's what life's about. I've told the players I have no fear about a game of football and I want them to have the same philosophy.'

McDermott was further buoyed by a final day victory against promotion-chasing Watford. He was convinced that he had a decent side at his disposal.

GFH Capital couldn't provide a massive transfer budget but found enough for McDermott to secure Leeds' first million-pound signing since Richard Cresswell in 2005. United beat off strong competition from Blackburn and Wolves to land highly rated Crewe midfielder Luke Murphy. They also brought in former Reading front man Noel Hunt, towering Oldham striker Matt Smith and Manchester United's utility defender, Scott Wootton.

McDermott had hoped for more but reconciled himself to the financial realities of life under GFH. He had seen enough at the end of the previous season to give him hope that he could turn Leeds into genuine promotion contenders.

The fans shared his optimism, their mood boosted by the news that the link with Ken Bates had been severed completely.

GFH had agreed to his continuing involvement under duress. They eagerly seized on the opportunity to banish him after learning that he had committed the club to a contract to fly him regularly to Leeds from his Monaco home. The three-year deal would cost £500,000.

Ever since he first took control at Elland Road, Bates had used a private jet for his trips from Monaco to Leeds and he insisted that his Leeds contract allowed him to continue to charge expenses at the previous level. He did not seek the approval of the board for the new contract and was unrepentant, threatening to take GFH Capital to court when they sacked him.

In the post-Bates world, the first game of the season, at home to Brighton, attracted 33,000 supporters eager to celebrate the demise of the former owner. They saw Leeds win the game but only thanks to a dramatic stoppage-time winner by Murphy on his debut.

Leeds built on the start with good results over the course of the first month, but after their first defeat, at home to QPR on 31 August, they lost four of the next five and slithered down the table to fifteenth, seemingly set for another disappointing season.

McDermott demanded an improvement when Leeds hosted Bournemouth on 1 October and was relieved when Dominic Poleon's goal with ten minutes remaining secured victory. Bournemouth had to play almost an hour with ten men after Ryan Allsop was sent off for conceding a penalty for a foul on Noel Hunt. Ross McCormack missed the spot kick and Leeds struggled to make their man advantage count.

'The only thing that mattered was to get the win,' commented McDermott. 'I was very happy to see us get over the line because we haven't won for a while and we desperately needed to win.'

Leeds tottered through an uncertain autumn but found enough points to climb to fifth by Christmas. Few supporters could quite see how they'd managed it. They still respected McDermott but were disappointed that the original promise of his reign hadn't led to greater progress.

The team had a dreadful time of things in December and January with five straight defeats including one at home to Blackburn, a shock FA Cup exit at Rochdale and the embarrassment of a 6-0 hammering at Sheffield Wednesday. As Leeds plunged to twelfth, the fans began to loudly voice doubts about the manager, but soon they would be united around him once more.

CHAPTER SEVENTEEN
Cellino

It had been obvious for months that GFH Capital were not at Leeds for the long haul. Despite all their fine words, the bank's only interest in Leeds was publicity and the opportunity of a big profit when they cashed in their shares. Being associated with a club that continued to potter away in the lower half of England's second tier did not fit with their plans and they had neither the money nor the experience to deal with the reality of the situation.

They touted around for 'strategic investors', betraying the fact that despite their lengthy due diligence, they simply did not have the backers they thought they could muster. Now they pushed in earnest, seemingly ready to consider a total buyout on the right terms.

It was apparent that Haigh had other motives, intent on a more meaningful relationship with Leeds United. He had grown frustrated at the haphazard nature of GFH's ownership and began to plan a rescue mission. He set up a company called Sport Capital to buy out GFH. In October, Haigh had arranged a six-figure loan to Leeds through his Berrydale Seventh Sport Holdings vehicle and now offered further cash injections to keep Leeds going as he prepared a bid.

He enlisted the help and support of others. Andrew Flowers, chairman and managing director of Enterprise Insurance, leading sponsors of the club, was one of those involved in Sport Capital. Emboldened by Flowers' interest, Haigh negotiated an exclusivity agreement with GFH and agreed a deal to buy 75 per cent of the shares. He blithely talked up the repurchase of Elland Road and negotiations for the return of Max Gradel to the club.

At the start of January, it was reported that Sport Capital's proposals had got as far as being forwarded to the Football League for their consideration, while the consortium claimed to have already forwarded £6 million to support the club's day-to-day operations.

Suddenly a rival bidder entered the reckoning. TogetherLeeds, a consortium headed by Welcome to Yorkshire chief executive Gary Verity and Mike Farnan, former MD of Manchester United International, enjoyed the backing of former Leeds captain Lucas Radebe. His status as a United legend earned brownie points with the fans. Farnan, well-respected for his work at Old Trafford, quickly put together a strong bid team.

TogetherLeeds tabled an offer of £7 million for an 80 per cent stake but GFH laughed in their faces, adamant that the offer undervalued the club.

Both consortia were taken completely unawares when a third bidder emerged, the Italian agricultural entrepreneur Massimo Cellino. He had made a fortune in the corn industry and was the owner of Cagliari, the club he had supported as a boy. He was known to be an avid football man but his past was chequered – he had been embroiled in a number of financial misdemeanours and there were accusations of tax evasion. He was also eccentric and impulsive, dispensing with the services of thirty-six managers during his twenty-two years at Cagliari.

The comedy of errors that epitomised Cellino's attempts to build a new ground for Cagliari ended in a bizarre period of house arrest after accusations of embezzlement, charges that appeared spurious and politically motivated.

Haigh had sought out Cellino to advise him on his proposed buyout, but it piqued the Italian's interest and soon he was considering making an approach of his own.

When he heard that Cellino had opened discussions with GFH, Flowers furiously denounced the Italian as a serial fraudster and attacked the bank for engaging with him, in contravention of the exclusivity contract. He revealed that Sport Capital had reduced their offer to GFH because 'a number of things have come to light which were not as originally described'. He added, 'We are convinced [Cellino] will not be in the interests of the club, the manager, the players or the fans. We must ask the question whether the prospective preferred bidder understands anything about the culture of Leeds United, its fans, its heritage or British football … As lifelong fans, we believe our offer and plans were in the best interests of the club and its loyal supporters. This boils down to much more than money but GFH have chosen to ignore that. We believe the owners have breached their covenant with us but much more importantly they have breached their covenant with the fans.'

Despite all Flowers' protestations and the potential ramifications, GFH had little compunction in pursuing agreements on all fronts. The bank appeared to favour Cellino's offer and the Italian and his representatives were often seen around Elland Road and Thorp Arch. A 75 per cent buyout neared agreement.

There were ominous events which boded ill – Cellino tried to foist Gianluca Festa, his preferred choice as coach, onto McDermott. The manager saw the move as a blatant attempt to undermine his authority and rejected the request out of hand.

Bizarrely, with his deal not yet done, Cellino told his lawyer, Chris Farnell, to tell McDermott on the eve of United's 1 February game that he had been sacked. He was acting beyond his authority, but McDermott took Farnell at his word and prepared to move on. Cellino ordered Academy manager Neil Redfearn to support Festa in arrangements for the Huddersfield fixture.

That evening was written into Elland Road legend as 'Mad Friday'. It was the final day of January's transfer window and there was an unseemly dispute over the future of talismanic striker Ross McCormack, with Leeds rejecting several offers from Cardiff and elsewhere.

The Scot had agreed to stay at Leeds but that was before he heard about McDermott's dismissal. The two had formed a bond and McCormack was devastated, telling Sky Sports, 'It's sad times at the club and I'm absolutely gutted because I had a really good relationship with the manager. I was looking forward to helping the club move forward under Brian McDermott and he made me captain. I'm very happy and content at the club but a big part of that was Brian McDermott … Brian was a little bit surprised in terms of how quick it has happened but he always had an inkling. The new owners are coming and want to take it in a different direction. If I'd known that this was going to happen, I'd have had a right decision to make.'

The combination of McDermott's sacking and McCormack's unrest provoked strong feelings among the supporters. In double-quick time, hundreds high-tailed it down to Elland Road and furiously demanded to see Cellino. The fans blockaded the car park, prompting urgent pleas from Stanningley Cars to 'let our taxi driver leave, the driver wants to go home, and he is close to running out of petrol'.

United shirt sponsors Enterprise Insurance dramatically withdrew its support and Academy sponsors Flamingo Land quickly followed suit.

Enterprise had paid a significant sponsorship fee up front, the money used to tie McCormack down to a new four-year contract in August. Flowers told the *Yorkshire Evening Post*, 'I'm devastated for Brian and we'll be looking to end our sponsorship of the club. In no way do we wish to be associated with this regime.'

After hours of sitting blithely on their hands, GFH Capital finally deigned to intervene. They restored McDermott, Haigh ringing to give him his full backing and asking him to take charge of the Huddersfield game. A shocked McDermott refused, although he was content to resume his position after the weekend.

McDermott's assistant Nigel Gibbs agreed to deputise, supported by Neil Redfearn. They reinstated McDermott's original selection and formation, which Festa had wanted to scrap.

The Huddersfield game was a passionate affair, with Leeds finding the form and spirit they had been hiding so long. They fought back from a goal behind to triumph 5-1, their performance lit up by a hat-trick from McCormack. The fans bellowed support for McDermott, rejection of Cellino and derision at the actions of GFH. 'Shoes off if you hate GFH' they sang loudly through the game, among some more pointed anthems.

It was difficult to see how the club could recover from such chaos, but McDermott was back on the Monday, conducting a press conference and clearly delighted at the show of supporter loyalty. He glowed with pride as he talked of the passion of Leeds' followers and the future of the club.

The team struggled to maintain their show of strength and meandered through a depressing spring, with heavy defeats at home to Bolton and Reading and away to Bournemouth and Watford. They trailed in a disappointing fifteenth.

McDermott and the players were forced to go without wages while Cellino and GFH bickered over who was responsible for the bill. Cellino, still waiting for his takeover to be ratified by the EFL, wouldn't take responsibility for the matter. GFH just sat with their collective feet up, seemingly oblivious to the issue. Even worse, nobody bothered to brief the staff – they had a nasty shock when the money didn't come through.

Cellino completed the purchase of the club but things were thrown into the melting pot when the Football League refused to accept him. On 24 March, the League revealed that he had failed their Owners' and Directors' Test after being found guilty in Sardinia of avoiding import duties of €388,500 on Nélie, a yacht seized by Italian police and customs officials in June 2012. The Italian court fined him €600,000, ordered him to pay legal costs and confiscated the yacht.

Cellino immediately appealed the decision, saying, 'I have to appeal. I feel a responsibility to the fans who I am proud to say wanted me. There are hours, not the next few days. Leeds needs help, needs blood, needs money. Leeds can't wait. What worries me is I am the only one worrying about that. It's embarrassing. I am not worrying about the money I have already paid and maybe am going to lose. I am feeling embarrassed, ashamed and down. It's not nice to say. I feel lost. I am not a crook. I didn't come to Leeds to do anything bad.'

In the face of the uncertainty, GFH and Cellino continued to argue over the payroll, each insisting that it was the other's responsibility. Cellino blinked first, agreeing to fund half of the salary bill pending his appeal and the players agreed to a partial deferral.

There were rumours that Ken Bates was still hovering in the background. He denied plans to launch a takeover bid but admitted being ready to put £1.5 million into Sport Capital though discussions came to nothing.

It was known that TogetherLeeds were also still circling, saying they were prepared to step in if Cellino's purchase failed. They claimed to have raised £36 million.

Farnan eventually admitted defeat. He said months later, 'We had some great plans for the club in terms of where we wanted to take it. I had a team of people that were exceptional in what they do, and what they could do if we got hold of the club.' Farnan and his team had spent eighteen months negotiating with GFH. 'Leeds fans are the most passionate fans in world football. I've been abused on Twitter, my link to Manchester United kind of got me a hard time. They are very passionate; they believe in the football club. I believe in Leeds as a city; I think it's fantastic.'

The news broke on 5 April that Cellino's appeal had been successful. After being cleared to press ahead with his buyout, his first act was to dismiss Haigh as managing director. Promising he would steer Leeds United back to the Premier League within two years, Cellino celebrated the takeover with fans at the Old Peacock pub across the road from the stadium.

Haigh was reinstated but swiftly departed after a dispute with Cellino over the installation of covert surveillance cameras in the boardroom and toilets. 'I am left with no alternative than to resign as managing director of the club,' said Haigh. 'This is a matter of particular regret to me since I was the person who first introduced Eleonora Sport to the club's owners. I also gave them my full and constant support in the Football League's lengthy approval process. As is well known by those in or close to the club, my unstinting support of Leeds United throughout my time at the club has extended to loaning the club money to ensure that tax, players and staff were paid and to underpin its continuing viability – loans which to this day remain in the club.'

The euphoria of buying Leeds United did not last long. Reality set in when the club published its accounts – 2011's profit of £1.6 million had been replaced by a £10.6 million loss under GFH. There was a forecast that this would rise to almost £23 million in the current year.

Cellino had no alternative other than to slash and burn – he brought in a team of specialist consultants to lead a cost-cutting exercise. One of the first measures was the temporary closure of Thorp Arch, the club's training facility. The revolution gathered pace with the announcement that there would be up to seventy redundancies. Ken Bates had eased his way in, retaining the services of Peter Lorimer, but Cellino was a man in a hurry – Lorimer was sacked, along with match day hosts Eddie Gray and Dominic Matteo.

CHAPTER EIGHTEEN
The Italian Job

'I'm going to talk to Brian,' said Cellino. 'We will speak to each other 100 per cent and I will speak to him honestly. There is so much going on at Leeds and already I've changed my mind ten times about a lot of things. But let me tell you, the coach is my last problem here.'

Despite his return to the fold, Brian McDermott was widely rumoured to be on borrowed time at Elland Road. Asked if he had approached potential replacements for the manager, Cellino dismissed the suggestion out of hand yet courted Benito Carbone, the former Bradford City and Sheffield Wednesday player.

Carbone, who retired in 2010, gave up his job coaching Italian side Saint Christophe Valle D'Aosta when he was approached by Cellino. He was all set to relocate to England though Cellino said it would be an unpaid role in the short term, seemingly unconcerned about the impact of Carbone's appointment on Neil Redfearn and other members of the Academy staff.

McDermott said he had spoken to Carbone before United's senior squad travelled to play Birmingham on 26 April but had not a clue as to what his role entailed.

The news set the headlines spinning with intense speculation that Carbone had been earmarked to replace McDermott.

The manager refused to engage with the gossip but before the final game of the season, at home to Derby, he insisted that he would exit United with pride in his performance and his head held high if the game was his last as manager. McDermott defended his record but gave no insight into his future.

He acknowledged the paucity of form in the second half of the season but insisted that he had been right to stand by the club.

'Things started to go wrong but did I handle that situation? Yes, without a doubt in my opinion. It would have been very easy to walk away on the first of February, but I was never going to do that and I'm glad and proud that I didn't. I didn't even think about it.

'We had a poor run for three months and you accept that. I don't want to talk about what's gone on off the pitch because it sounds like excuses ... But since the club's been stable, we've won three out of the last four games.

'People have opinions on everything but I've tried to be absolutely honest in everything I've done. I've tried to tell the truth as I see it and I've not ducked anything.'

McDermott said there were no plans for discussions with Cellino and admitted he had no way of knowing if he would still be manager after the summer.

'I must be 100 per cent confident in my coach at the start of the season,' Cellino told BBC Radio Leeds. 'I must have a coach that is very good on the field and helps me manage by choosing players ... We have to let things cool down. Maybe in a week or ten days' time both of us will be ready to talk about the future. We are engaged in another two years of contract and that is also very important for us because we cannot waste money changing ... Me and Brian have to sort it out very fairly and in a sporting way.'

The schism between Cellino and McDermott deepened over the summer with the Italian accusing the coach of being absent without leave. He was actually visiting his mother in hospital but an uncaring Cellino ordered him and the staff to return to Elland Road weeks ahead of the scheduled date. He was clearly trying to provoke a reaction but McDermott held his peace and refused to give Cellino an easy way out. Their dispute was brought to an end after weeks of argument when the two men agreed to cancel the manager's contract by mutual consent.

There was endless speculation about who would replace McDermott. Glib forecasts from 'those in the know' that Carbone would be the new man in charge were abruptly proven wrong by Cellino. He severed contacts with his 'special consultant' at the beginning of August after springing a surprise with the appointment of his new head coach.

It was a total unknown, former Forest Green Rovers boss David Hockaday, who emerged from obscurity to rapidly become the bookies' favourite. He was duly revealed as the new man on 19 June to the astonishment of virtually everyone.

Hockaday had received a call from one of Cellino's representatives asking if he would be interested in meeting his client, whom he declined to identify. Based on the Italian accent, Hockaday assumed that the club in question was either Leeds or Leyton Orient. The O's were also under new Italian ownership after long-time owner Barry Hearn sold his 90 per cent stake to Italian businessman Francesco Becchetti. Hockaday did his homework on both clubs.

A clandestine meeting was arranged, all cloak and dagger. Cellino and Hockaday talked football for about five hours and the Italian warmed to his guest. Cellino said, 'I really like the way you think – would you like to be head coach at Leeds United?'

Hockaday was shocked, he had thought Cellino wanted an assistant manager or an Academy coach. He was initially reticent, saying, 'I've got a reputation as a decent coach – but the Leeds fans and the media will be saying, "David who?" Are you prepared for that?'

The headstrong Cellino was steadfast and quickly made Hockaday an offer he simply couldn't refuse.

Hockaday was well aware of Cellino's record with coaches but just could not resist the opportunity. His hope was that Leeds would bring in some decent players and he would be given a fair run at the job.

Cellino, who declared that 'the town has a new sheriff', closed Thorp Arch over the summer months, closed its laundry and insisted that players had to bring in their own packed lunches. The players were ordered back to Elland Road early with several having to cancel their holidays, despite not having received their wages after a winding-up order was lodged against the club.

In an attempt to boost team spirit, Cellino introduced a rule dictating where the players could live. 'Next season I do not want one single player who lives outside of Leeds, no way. That is mandatory,' he told BBC Radio Leeds. 'Last year there were players who were coming late to games. Next year before a home game the players will stay together, have dinner together and go to the game together.'

He also decreed that after away games the players would travel back to Leeds together. Even if a game was on a player's home turf, they were banned from visiting friends and family.

Hockaday's recruitment suggestions fell largely on deaf ears. 'I said we needed a leader. Cardiff said we could have Mark Hudson for free, but Cellino said, "No, I don't fancy him, who else?" I said, "There's a lad at Celtic, Virgil van Dijk, and there's a lad called Craig Cathcart." He wasn't interested in any of those, then brought in Giuseppe Bellusci.

'Liverpool were prepared to give us Conor Coady for nothing, but he said, "Too young" … We did sign Liam Cooper from Chesterfield, though – that recommendation was listened to.'

Hockaday sanctioned the sale of Ross McCormack to Fulham for £11 million and new director of football Nicola Salerno began rebuilding the squad, fishing extensively in Italy's Serie B. There was a clutch of obscure Europeans, a few home-grown players and Brazilian wonder kid Adryan.

The quality of the newcomers disappointed Hockaday. He feared that they wouldn't be up to the job but couldn't persuade Cellino to take a different route. He derided the squad as dysfunctional, his job made all the more

The Italian Job

challenging when Cellino informed all the senior players they were on the way out.

Hockaday was asked to transform Cellino's rag bag army into a team ready to thrive in the notoriously competitive environment of the Championship. He failed dismally, sacked by Cellino after six games, the appointment conceded as flawed.

The pedigree of Hockaday's replacement, Sturm Graz coach Darko Milanic, was better, but when asked about his qualities, all Cellino could say was 'He's good-looking.'

The relationship between the two quickly turned sour and Milanic lasted just six games and thirty-two days which included not a single win. He was sacked by Cellino, who admitted, 'I made a mistake with this guy. He is negative, he has a losing mentality. He has three points from six games, that is relegation [form].'

A spurned Milanic bitterly insisted that he was merely on gardening leave and would return to Elland Road at a time to be specified.

Cellino turned to Academy manager Neil Redfearn, who had enjoyed some success when he acted as caretaker manager in the interregnum between Hockaday and Milanic. Cellino declared, 'I hope he's going to stay at Leeds for the next ten years.'

Redfearn had the twin advantages of being adored by the fans and possessing the knack of coaxing some decent performances out of the players. Things were helped by the rich promise of the Academy with Byram, Taylor, Cook and Mowatt making impressive contributions, much to the liking of the fans, who loved home-grown youngsters.

It wasn't an easy road and five defeats in six games led to Leeds plunging to twenty-first position by 10 January. The appointment of Steve Thompson as assistant to Redfearn before Christmas reaped rewards as Leeds put together a decent string of results, three successive victories in February taking them up to eleventh. Redfearn had to fight tooth and nail to bring in Thompson.

Some of the upturn was down to the absence of Cellino, who was banned again by the League on 1 December after they received detailed evidence from the Italian court that convicted him of tax evasion. He had to stand away from the club until March, when the conviction would be considered spent. Insisting that he would not sell his shares in the club, Cellino handed over the chairmanship to banker Andrew Umbers in the meantime.

LUST questioned the League's motives regarding the timing, arguing that it would cause maximum disruption to any plans for the transfer window. LUST suggested that the League should have concentrated on 'redeveloping their outdated Owners' and Directors' Test so that it is more robust and fit for purpose. Times have changed over the last ten years and there are countless examples of the test failing to address modern-day ownership issues with the current situation at Leeds United being the latest of these.

'Does it really make sense for the Football League to continue to spend time and resources pursuing the Nélie situation when their best-case outcome is a three-month ban from control of the club? Rather than demonstrating a determination to stamp out rogue behaviour it appears to the general public more as a witch hunt to satisfy their bruised egos.'

Cellino faced other setbacks. He promised to buy back Elland Road, but his efforts were stymied by United's financial track record. He could have financed the deal himself but declined to do so because it would have been pouring money down the greedy gullets of GFH Capital. They sat back and allowed Cellino to take all the risks while the value of their shares grew.

Nevertheless, Cellino was successful in wringing £5 million out of GFH as he himself ploughed in a further £15 million. It needed several visits to Bahrain to agree the deal.

The scale of losses under GFH saw the club hit by a transfer embargo. It had not been unexpected and was the reason why United's transfer activity had been so extensive in the summer. They had bought in eleven men permanently with another four on loan deals. There were loopholes in the League's ban and during January Leeds signed Sol Bamba, Granddi Ngoyi and Edgar Cani on loan, although only Bamba had any real impact.

When the League threatened further sanctions against Cellino, the Italian agreed to accept the extension of his exclusion until the beginning of May to put an end to the matter, but he was seething inside, furious at what he saw as petty-mindedness.

He continued to pull the strings behind the scenes and took against Redfearn, seemingly jealous of the coach's relationship with the supporters. Cellino engineered a dispute between Thompson and Salerno that led to the departure of both men. In the aftermath, United's form collapsed and they lost five games in a row, although they finished well clear of the relegation zone.

Redfearn hoped that he would remain in charge for 2015/16, but his expectations were dashed when Cellino returned from his exile and gave him a public slating for being 'weak' and 'a baby'. Redfearn recognised that the writing was on the wall long before he became the fifth United coach dismissed by Cellino in little more than a year.

In his stead came former Brentford and Wigan manager Uwe Rosler, a forty-seven-year-old German, who first came to the fore as a dynamic striker with Manchester City.

This was a man with genuine managerial experience and a track record, hinting that Cellino had finally got the message and recognised the need for a known quantity if he was to achieve his stated aim of promotion to the Premier League.

He also enlisted the support of Adam Pearson as executive director, a man who had served as United's commercial director until 2001. He brought a cool, diligent air to proceedings and appeared to bring the best out in Cellino.

Reassured by the presence of such an experienced management team, Cellino put money up to give Rosler a fighting chance of promotion. Sol Bamba's contract was made permanent for £1 million and then Rosler paid out £5.3 million to boost his attacking resources with deals for Chris Wood, Stuart Dallas and Jordan Botaka.

It was a calm and steady period after the frenetic chaos of a year earlier under Hockaday and the fans began to believe that a corner might have been turned.

Unfortunately, Rosler couldn't transform all the potential and confidence into results on the field and his eleven Championship games produced just two victories and nine goals.

Brighton's victory at Elland Road on 17 October was the third defeat in a row and was the last straw for Cellino, who summarily terminated Rosler's contract.

'I watched the game on Saturday and in the second half, we were just trying not to lose,' Cellino told the *Daily Mirror*. 'We were not trying to win. That is not good enough. I wanted them to play heavy rock football but instead it was like country music. I did my best to help Uwe, but in the end, I could not see even a patch of blue in the sky, just cloud, cloud and cloud.'

Cellino took issue with Rosler's comment a week earlier that his side was not good enough to win promotion. 'Why did he say that? The fans want to dream, so why did he say that? To say that after eleven or twelve games is wrong. That is not right for the fans.'

Cellino instantly appointed Rotherham manager Steve Evans. It was his final act as chairman for quite a while. Hours later the Football League disqualified him for twelve months following a conviction for tax evasion in Italy.

As the club was ushered towards an uncertain future, it appeared there was no end to the cruel tricks that fate had in store for Leeds United.

CHAPTER NINETEEN

Becalmed

The first eighteen months of Massimo Cellino's ownership of Leeds United will be remembered as a whirlwind of chaos with the Italian living up to his reputation for eccentricity. He dispensed with five managers and his recruitment of Steve Evans was considered by many only marginally less bizarre than that of Dave Hockaday. Evans was initially regarded as a joke of cosmic proportions, and few people welcomed the Glaswegian bruiser with any elation.

Gradually, however, Evans won some supporters round and earned grudging respect for the steadying hand he brought to the tiller. He found enough form and points to make 2015/16 an uneventful season with hints of neither promotion nor relegation – all that could really be hoped for in the circumstances. There was never any way Evans was going to be given the opportunity to take Leeds on to the next level, however, and Cellino cut him adrift in the summer with an absence of either gratitude or respect.

The uncertainty left a distraught Evans stumbling tearfully through a press conference after the penultimate game at Preston.

The Italian was in a resigned mood himself, wearied by his disputes with the League and demoralised by protests from the fans. They had upped the ante with mock funerals for him as they chanted 'Time to Go Massimo' and projected messages of protest onto the side of the East Stand. #TTGM became de rigueur on social media as the strapline for a very active campaign against his continued ownership. Cellino's disqualification as a director was set aside pending an appeal, but the wind had unquestionably gone from his sails.

He claimed that he was ready to sell his shares in the club to Leeds Fans United, a Community Benefit Society representing the supporters, and then told the world he would no longer attend United games. They were decisions born of deep frustration and high emotion and he quickly changed his mind on both counts, though he insisted that if he could get the right offer, he would walk away from the club.

Steve Parkin came back into the picture with an offer to buy 51 per cent of the club for £25 million. He claimed later that contracts were hours away from being signed before Cellino went cold on the deal. Parkin revealed that his due diligence identified that the Italian had put £45 million of his own money into the club by that stage.

Shortly after the discussions with Parkin ran into the ground, a new man came onto the scene. Italian sports media entrepreneur Andrea Radrizzani won Cellino's confidence and persuaded him that he was a man with whom he could do business. There was a meeting of the minds after Radrizzani contacted Cellino to discuss getting involved in the project.

Agreement was reached on the sale of 50 per cent of Cellino's shares and the transaction was completed in January 2017. Radrizzani also secured the option of a full takeover if Leeds failed to achieve promotion at the end of the season. The value of the club was set at £44.8 million.

At the time, promotion seemed a decent bet with Garry Monk, appointed head coach in June 2016, overcoming a difficult opening month to lead Leeds to a strong position.

A single-goal defeat at home to Huddersfield left Leeds third from bottom on 10 September, with just three points from six games. In a normal season, Cellino would have instantly handed Monk his P45, but Radrizzani persuaded him to hang fire, a decision that paid dividends as Leeds won sixteen of the following twenty-three games.

After Radrizzani completed the purchase of half of the share capital, he and Cellino gave a press conference on 14 January to explain their plans.

The previous evening, Leeds had performed admirably to beat Derby County. The points saw United climb to third in the table. Momentum was with them, despite the dominance of Brighton and Newcastle at the top of the table.

Monk was delighted with the fruits of his labour. He had substantially refurbished the side, fashioning a new spine. Former West Ham, QPR and England keeper Rob Green was protected by Kyle Bartley of Swansea and Torino's Swedish international Pontus Jansson. Monk brought in Spanish playmaker Pablo Hernandez, Bristol City right-back Luke Ayling and Oxford forward Kemar Roofe. His entire approach was built around the strengths of Chris Wood. The New Zealand international striker found incredible form in front of goal. Much of the credit was laid at the door of former Southampton and England front man James Beattie, a key member of Monk's coaching team.

Wood got off the mark in his second game and ended the campaign with thirty goals, twenty-seven of them in the Championship, making him the division's leading scorer. Hernandez was the architect of much of Leeds' football, granted the freedom of the park by Liam Bridcutt's solidity in midfield as Vieira, Phillips, Dallas and O'Kane rotated around them. United were also stronger at the back where they boasted the division's third best defensive record.

Hadi Sacko, Kemar Roofe and Souleymane Doukara brought an erratic attacking presence but the latter pulled off perhaps the finest volley that United fans had witnessed since Tony Yeboah in 1995.

With fifteen minutes to go in the game against Nottingham Forest on 25 January, Doukara unleashed an unstoppable strike from outside the box. Forest goalkeeper Stephen Henderson dived, but the velocity of the ball was such that no goalkeeper in the world could have saved it.

That was a rare highlight in Doukara's stay at Leeds. He scored fourteen goals in three years after a £1.5 million move from Catania.

It was a surprise when Monk declined to strengthen significantly in the January window, limiting himself to two wingers on loan – Reading's Mo Barrow and Alfonso Pedraza from Villareal. Only the latter had an impact as consistency disappeared. He was an electrifying presence, wrapping up a victory at Birmingham on 3 March with a powerful strike into the bottom corner.

A month earlier, Leeds had come unstuck in a feisty derby away to promotion rivals Huddersfield. The Terriers' German centre-back, Michael Hefele, netted the decisive goal a minute from the end, prompting a violent coming together of the two coaches. Monk seethed with anger as Huddersfield manager David Wagner celebrated too enthusiastically. He shoved the German slyly as he ran past. That resulted in a mass confrontation with two men from each side booked and both coaches sent to the stands.

'I really felt for my players at the end,' said Monk. 'They didn't deserve that at all; they deserved at least a point today. I thought we were very committed, we disrupted them, we followed a good game plan and our display warranted more than what we got. It was a bitter pill to swallow.'

The result saw Huddersfield leapfrog Leeds into fourth and Cardiff's victory at Elland Road the following week further sapped morale.

Monk managed to coax a seven-game unbeaten spell, culminating in a 2-0 defeat of second-placed Brighton courtesy of two second-half goals from Wood. The points lifted Leeds to fourth, eight points behind the Seagulls, and opened an eight-point cushion to Fulham just outside the top six with eight games to go.

The advantage should have been decisive but the promotion charge was undermined two weeks later by a narrow defeat at Reading, who swapped places with Leeds as a consequence.

Defeat at Brentford was another nail in the coffin, but Leeds bounced back with a 3-0 hammering of eighth-placed Preston. They took the lead when Roofe kept his cool to lift his shot over keeper Chris Maxwell and then Hernandez made it 2-0 on the stroke of half-time.

Preston were unlucky when Tom Barkhuizen's shot struck the bar before Alex Baptiste saw red for kicking Hernandez off the ball.

Substitute Doukara finished well to seal victory in the last minute and Leeds regained their cushion of five points on seventh place with five games to go.

Sadly, those fixtures yielded a mere three points and Monk's men ended five points outside the play-offs.

It was the best finish since Simon Grayson achieved the same feat in 2011, but bitterly disappointing after being fixtures in the top six from the end of November until mid-April.

Their hopes were all but ended in the penultimate game. Leeds fought back from a three-goal deficit at home to Norwich to snatch a 3-3 draw, but it was not enough.

'It's difficult to be critical of the group as we've said for so long how much they've given to the club,' said Monk afterwards. 'The reality is the majority of the group were not quite ready for this situation ... That's not a criticism, it's just a fact.

'I have one more game left, I'll be focused on that. The club have said when they want to speak, I have to respect that. Even when that comes, it's us both agreeing on how we take this forward. I have my views and the club will have theirs.'

Those were ominous words – Monk left for Middlesbrough despite Leeds' attempt to extend his contract.

By then, it was Radrizzani in charge after he secured full control of the club, buying Cellino's remaining shares after it was confirmed that Leeds were set for another year in the Championship.

News of Monk's departure came as a bitter disappointment for fans but they were jumping up and down on 23 May when Radrizzani repurchased the Elland Road stadium, thirteen years after it had been sold by Adulant Force.

It cost him £20 million to secure the deeds from Teak Commercial Limited, an offshore firm which had been charging United an annual rent of around £1.7 million.

Many self-proclaimed saviours had pledged they would restore ownership of Elland Road to Leeds but it was Radrizzani who quietly and calmly did the trick without any song and dance. The transaction was of huge symbolic importance, marking the return of stability to Leeds United after a decade and a half of chaos and mismanagement.

Plainly, Radrizzani was a man who meant business.

CHAPTER TWENTY

New Kids on the Block

With Cellino's part in the Elland Road story consigned to history, Andrea Radrizzani had free rein to develop his plans. He had spent a year shadowing his predecessor, observing how things worked and had done his homework well. He was desperate to restore order to a club that had spent fifteen years in financial meltdown and knew he had a major rebuilding task on his hands. He needed to bring in a new management team and rebuild the squad after the departure of some of Monk's key men.

Kyle Bartley returned to parent club Swansea and by the end of the transfer window, Charlie Taylor, Chris Wood, Liam Bridcutt and Rob Green had all gone, along with the last vestiges of Cellino's reign with Giuseppe Bellusci, Marco Silvestri, Lee Erwin and Souleymane Doukara finding new homes.

Radrizzani was clear about both his vision and what was needed to realise it. Like Cellino, he favoured the European model with a management team consisting of a director of football, a chief executive and a head coach, but he was no dictator. He wanted people who could make a positive contribution, who were prepared to stand up to him.

His first step was bringing in the Spaniard Victor Orta as director of football and a month later he appointed West Ham managing director Angus Kinnear as chief executive. They were men with strong track records, Orta with an unrivalled contact list and knowledge of the European leagues, and Kinnear with capabilities on the financial and commercial side. He had previously worked at Arsenal in a similar capacity, overseeing the move to the Emirates Stadium. They made a good team.

Orta's recruitment from Middlesbrough prompted many to think that the new coach would be former Boro man Aitor Karanka, but Radrizzani had other ideas.

He had bought into Cellino's view that the coach was the least important component of the management team, there to get the best out of the resources available to him, not to shape things. He sprang a shock by appointing an unknown Dane, Thomas Christiansen. Radrizzani was swayed by Christiansen's enthusiasm, attention to detail and readiness to leave player recruitment to Orta. That was something which Monk had strongly objected to and was a key factor in his decision to jump ship.

There was a logic to the appointment. Happy to work within Radrizzani's management structure, Christiansen combined youth with a decent amount of experience.

Orta made massive changes to the first-team pool over the summer, although he spent as much time replenishing the development squad.

Pontus Jansson's transfer from Torino was made permanent for £3.6 million and winger Hadi Sacko's loan was also converted at a cost of £1.5 million. Orta raided the European mainland to bring in Mateusz Klich, Felix Wiedwald, Vurnon Anita, Caleb Ekuban, Samu Saiz, Gianni Alioski, Jay-Roy Grot and Pawel Cibicki at a combined cost of £11 million. Matthew Pennington, Cameron Borthwick-Jackson and Pierre-Michel Lasogga signed on loan.

Such wholesale change was bound to take a while to bed in, but Christiansen seemed to have the magic touch. He was buoyed by an excellent opening run, five victories from the first seven games as Leeds secured the Championship leadership with a 2-0 defeat of Birmingham on 12 September.

He proclaimed, 'We are the team to beat,' without a hint of arrogance. Six consecutive Championship clean sheets had brought stability and an atmosphere of revival. The Dane understood that things could quickly change but he was convinced his team could cope with the status of favourites. 'My ideal of course is to dominate, to have control of the ball, to play offensive football, attractive but at the same time organised and good in defence … But also to be flexible … It's very important for a coach to have players who can adapt.'

Assessing Monk's side, Christiansen said he thought they were too dependent on Wood. He had attempted to galvanise his midfield to fill the gap left by the departure of the top scorer.

The Birmingham result was the high-water mark. Christiansen didn't exactly inspire confidence but enjoyed a huge portion of luck. A brittle edifice crumbled and eight defeats in the next eleven games saw Leeds drift down to tenth after losing 4-1 at Wolves on 22 November. The first reverse came at the hands of the 'in-yer-face' aggression of Millwall and ten days later, Neil Warnock's Cardiff City repeated the trick, crushing Leeds 3-1. The blueprint was swiftly adopted by other sides: pressurise goalkeeper Wiedwald and prevent the quick passes out, deny Leeds space in midfield and close mark the strikers.

Christiansen's tactical approach was rigid and inflexible; he had neither the solutions nor the leadership chutzpah to find a way out of the straitjacket he had donned.

Shorn of the opportunity for quick distribution, Wiedwald had few other assets to commend him and was quickly exposed as a nervous wreck by Championship strikers, flapping helplessly whenever the ball came within 5 yards of him. He lost his place after conceding three goals at Sheffield Wednesday, but reserve keeper Andy Lonergan was no solution, suffering his own nightmares.

Wiedwald was recalled after seven games but had not improved. The goal he conceded at QPR on 9 December was typical, allowing a 40-yard hoof to bounce over him and into the net. He wasn't far off his line but completely misjudged the flight of the ball. The error could have cost Leeds the game, but Roofe's hat-trick was enough to secure the first of four straight victories as Leeds made their way back up to fifth on Boxing Day.

The defeat at Birmingham that saw out 2017 ended the winning run and heralded a dispiriting ten-game winless streak. During that spell, Leeds lost at Newport in the FA Cup and conceded four at home to both Millwall and Cardiff. The latter game, on 3 February, broke Radrizzani's patience – the Bluebirds were 3-0 ahead at the break with Leeds down to ten men after Gaetano Berardi was sent off.

Leeds were tenth, seven points off the play-off pace with eight games remaining, and Radrizzani realised that it was now or never. He put Christiansen out of his misery, admitting that his appointment had been a mistake.

The Italian admitted he was 'really keen to change' the head coach at the beginning of January but was persuaded to hang fire by Orta. He said Christiansen 'probably lacked a little bit in terms of knowledge of the football,' adding, 'He needs to improve in terms of communication and leadership and confidence, which is a word I used a lot with him but it didn't improve.'

He accepted that with a new coach and so many new players, it was a good result to be in the top six for most of the season but declared Christiansen a failure. He criticised his decision-making during Christmas week when Leeds played four games with the same eleven or twelve players. 'This basically killed the players on the pitch and also killed the other ones because they were not considered. And then in the next game, in the Cup, Newport … asking the same players that were totally ignored for the four games in the League to play in the Cup against a Second Division side. Obviously, the commitment was not there because they were not considered before. So, in that two weeks I think we killed the season.'

New Kids on the Block

Radrizzani wasted no time in recruiting Christiansen's replacement, agreeing a contract with Barnsley head coach Paul Heckingbottom. In retrospect, it seemed needlessly hasty, with the Italian haphazardly diverting in an entirely new direction.

At first the pragmatic Heckingbottom seemed a good fit for the Leeds set-up but he was unable to get them back on track, tinkering endlessly with his selections as he struggled to find a spark of inspiration.

It was four games before his first win, and another five before his second. By then, Leeds were fourteenth, needing a miracle to get into the play-offs.

Heckingbottom had inherited a dysfunctional, dispirited and ill-disciplined squad. There had been four dismissals in Christiansen's final six games. Heckingbottom delved into the development squad for a solution, blooding Bailey Peacock-Farrell, Tom Pearce and Paudie O'Connor. It freshened things up but was no panacea.

There was widespread criticism of Orta's player recruitment with most of the newcomers dismissed as unsuitable for English football, impressive on YouTube but found badly wanting when it came to the real thing. Ekuban, Wiedwald, Cibicki, Grot and Laurens De Bock looked exactly what they were, expensive mistakes.

Radrizzani publicly slated the players after the 3-0 defeat at Middlesbrough at the start of March, questioning their commitment. 'We give them everything possible to just focus on the football … We gave them long-term contracts, we supported them in pre-season going on a camp in Spain, we did everything they wanted. But we didn't get back their commitment, their passion and spirit, particularly in the game, a really important game when we played really poorly against Middlesbrough. For me it was the bottom of the season because there was no commitment, no passion, no spirit.

'I don't want players in my team representing Leeds United with this behaviour. So I hope they can learn and be with me next year, playing better and with more commitment.'

Even two victories in the final three games could not paper over the cracks. Before that there had been a mere two wins in nineteen Championship matches. Heckingbottom was not the man to lead Radrizzani's revolution and the Italian conceded the error of his ways. Heckingbottom's contract was terminated on 1 June after another wasted season.

Clearly, this would not be as easy as Radrizzani had hoped and he had some hard thinking ahead of him.

CHAPTER TWENTY-ONE

The Genius on the Blue Bucket

In the old days, when Leeds United were one of the most respected clubs in Europe, they were led by some of the game's finest managers … Don Revie, Brian Clough, Jock Stein, Howard Wilkinson, George Graham, Terry Venables. It was years since United had gone hunting in a pool of such big fish.

Shaken by his failed experiments with unknown quantities, Andrea Radrizzani was determined to get a man who could make Leeds United tick when he set out to replace Paul Heckingbottom in the summer of 2018.

There were some big names on the Italians' list of possibles, but the man at the top of the list was less well-known to the run-of-the-mill football fan. Some of the world's most eminent coaches, though, certainly rated Marcelo Bielsa, a sixty-two-year-old Argentine who had led both Argentina and Chile in World Cup tournaments. Pep Guardiola, Mauricio Pochettino and Diego Simeone all freely acknowledged the debt they owed to Bielsa and how highly they rated him.

He had achieved extraordinary things with boyhood favourites Newell's Old Boys, Velez Sarsfield and Athletic Bilbao before less successful periods with Olympique Marseille, Lazio and Lille.

The episode with Lille ended in acrimony with Bielsa sacked after a dispute over transfers and the direction of the club. The matter had been subject to a legal case with Bielsa suing for €19 million in damages.

Victor Orta never thought Leeds would have a chance of capturing Bielsa when Radrizzani asked whom he considered the best man to take on his project but put forward his name regardless. When Radrizzani gave the nod, Orta set the wheels in motion.

It was not a question of persuading one of the globe's most revered coaches to take up the reins at Elland Road; it was all about allowing Bielsa to decide for himself that the revival of Leeds United, the archetypal sleeping giants, was a project worthy of his attention.

Bielsa quickly satisfied himself that this was indeed such a project, an emotion-soaked challenge that appealed to the instincts that had so endeared Newell's to him.

Bielsa was no ordinary coach and Leeds United was no ordinary club. Its name had been dragged through the mud, its history rubbished, its status dismissed as a thing of the past, but undoubtedly it was still a remarkable club, supported by remarkable fans and now owned by a remarkable man in Radrizzani. Bielsa would not manage just any old club; he had to be certain it was one with which he could empathise, in a city that he could identify with and which would fall in love with him.

And certainly, the people of Leeds fell in love with Bielsa in a way that they had not done with anyone since Don Revie. Howard Wilkinson came close when he captured the Second Division title and the league championship within two years of each other, but he lost his way and the love of the fans badly enough to be discarded four years later.

After weeks of courtship, Radrizzani got his man on 15 June, persuading Bielsa to sign a two-year contract with an option of a third. It cost a fortune with Bielsa becoming United's best paid manager ever at £6 million, twice the cost of any other Championship coach and half a million more than the Football Association paid Gareth Southgate.

'It has always been my ambition to work in England,' said Bielsa. 'I have had several opportunities to do so during my career, however I have always felt it was important to wait for the right project to come along ... when a club with Leeds United's history made me an offer, it was impossible to turn down.'

'He is a coach that I have admired for many years,' said Radrizzani. 'When the opportunity arose to bring him to Elland Road, we made it our top priority for the summer ... Marcelo has a wealth of experience and he will use that to create a new culture and a winning mentality at our football club.'

Angus Kinnear revealed that Bielsa's stated intention was to get the best out of the players already at Elland Road rather than bring in a mass of new recruits. He cited Liam Cooper and Kalvin Phillips as men whom Bielsa intended to develop into 'the best in the division'.

Leeds laid out £3 million to secure Wolves left-back Barry Douglas but Patrick Bamford of Middlesbrough was the marquee signing, his transfer fee set at an initial £7 million with the scope to climb to £10 million. It was the club's most expensive transfer since the purchase of Robbie Fowler in 2001. Bamford had put himself slam bang into the centre of United's vision with his hat-trick when Middlesbrough beat Heckingbottom's side in March.

Orta's insight into workings at the Riverside helped considerably and Bielsa was quickly sold on Bamford's benefits. He was perfect for the game that Bielsa wanted to play, someone who could fill the role of lone front runner in addition to scoring goals.

Bielsa was steadfast about his commitment to a small, tight squad. Twelve members of the first team and development squads departed permanently while another twenty were lent out. The greatest anguish came with fans' favourite Ronaldo Vieira sold to Sampdoria to help Leeds cope with the rules of Financial Fair Play.

It was an extraordinary cull, Bielsa clear that he did not want to have players with little chance of playing hanging around Elland Road. He was happy to rely on Academy players in the event of injury, a sharp break from previous practice.

Four players, three of them from Chelsea, were brought in on loan to add some depth, but only Manchester City wide man Jack Harrison had any genuine impact.

Pre-season was hard going, with Bielsa and his coaching team driving the players hard, intent on bringing them to peak fitness. The term 'Murderball' became a staple element of the Bielsa myth.

Mateusz Klich, the Polish midfielder who returned from loan to become a mainstay of Bielsa's United, gave some insight into the legendary training drill.

'It's basically playing 11 v 11 with no stops ... Constantly running around and sprinting, and you have all the coaches on the pitch screaming all the time and you can't stop running. It's just a normal game with normal rules ... You just play, but you can't stop running. It's tough, but it's the most important session in the week. It depends on the training how long he wants us to play. It could be five times six minutes, or one times twenty minutes. It just depends what Marcelo wants. Even if the ball goes out, there's a member of staff waiting with another ball to put it in. You can't stop.'

Certainly, by the time that the new season came around, the players' fitness was transformed. They were lean, mean and ready to run until they dropped.

Bielsa sprang several surprises on the opening day, although the adoption of a 4-1-4-1 formation was not one of them.

There were notable absentees from the starting XI in the shape of Chelsea loanee keeper Jamal Blackman, Pontus Jansson, Harrison and Bamford.

The most significant omission was Jansson, who had been allowed an extended absence following Sweden's participation in the World Cup finals. One of Bielsa's foibles was a refusal to select anyone whom he felt was not yet acclimatised to his regime. Jansson would not be the last player to experience the feeling.

Another surprise was the inclusion of Klich, whose Leeds career had appeared stillborn after Christiansen despatched him on loan the previous season. The absence through injury of Adam Forshaw and the sale of Vieira gave the Pole an early opportunity to prove he still had something to bring to the party.

Bielsa persisted with twenty-one-year-old Bailey Peacock-Farrell in goal, despite expectations that Blackman would be first choice. Heckingbottom had turned to Peacock-Farrell after the failure of both Wiedwald and Lonergan. He had seized the opportunity well enough to earn a first cap for Northern Ireland in May.

Douglas was the only new man in the starting eleven with Gaetano Berardi taking Jansson's place and Luke Ayling and Liam Cooper completing the back four.

Bielsa employed Kalvin Phillips as a holding midfielder, occasionally being withdrawn to make it three centre-backs – it was evident that the manager had worked closely with Phillips during the summer. The player was not entirely comfortable when Bielsa revealed his plans – Phillips as quarterback, capitalising on his ability to read the game and set moves in motion with long, raking passes.

Pablo Hernandez was used wide right in front of Klich with Samu Saiz filling the No. 10 role. Gianni Alioski was asked to drive up and down the left flank and Kemar Roofe led the line.

Leeds kicked the season off against relegated Stoke City, a team strongly fancied to go back up at the first attempt. Many thought United would struggle to contain them, even more so when they saw Bielsa's selection.

They should have known better. Bielsa hit the ground running and won 3-1, looking back not once after Klich opened the scoring in the fifteenth minute.

'I've never seen Leeds play like this,' said one overjoyed spectator, echoing the views of many of the happy faces around him.

The next game was even better, an extraordinary 4-1 victory at Derby County. Klich again set the ball rolling after five minutes and Roofe showed the Bielsa Effect, playing better than he ever had and scoring two breathtaking goals.

A year earlier, Christiansen had flattered to deceive, but Bielsa looked like a genuine Messiah in waiting. Bielsa's impact was extraordinary, coaxing wonderful performances from a squad that the previous year had looked distinctly average.

Rotherham were easy meat and Leeds squeezed a point out of Swansea before another superb display, away to Norwich. Klich's third goal of the season got the show on the road again and Leeds blossomed in the sunshine, making the Canaries look inept in a 3-0 hammering that was over long before Hernandez wrapped things up with the third goal after sixty-seven minutes.

The influence of the Spanish playmaker had quickly become evident to Bielsa.

'It's obvious that Hernandez has been very important to our team,' said the Argentine. 'He is the player who has the best regularity and he's the player with the biggest influence in the control of the games. He's a very intelligent player.'

Asked to expand on the importance of the Spaniard, Bielsa commented, 'I think he can make me a better head coach because I see solutions he is finding and decisions he is taking, that I only saw a very few times during my career.'

Some had expressed serious doubts about Bielsa, that he was a spent force with his best years behind him. They counselled that he would struggle to cope with the prosaic demands of Championship football, but they could not have been more wrong.

Unwilling to compromise, he imposed his commitment to attacking football and the intense press. He set the agenda rather than responding to it.

'We play football as she is meant to be played.'

After a delightful unbeaten opening run of eight games with four clean sheets, Leeds looked like they would coast to promotion. The fans glowed with excitement, but their confidence was shaken by three defeats in the nine fixtures that followed.

The last of those, by 4-1 at promotion rivals West Bromwich Albion on 10 November, appeared critical, as Leeds relinquished the leadership of the division to Norwich. Normal order was restored with a lengthy winning streak.

Two days before Christmas at Aston Villa, Leeds fell two goals behind after seventeen minutes. It looked like the run was done, but eighteen-year-old winger Jack Clarke came off the bench at half-time to inspire a blistering comeback. Eleven minutes in and Clarke came flying off the left flank to jink past several defenders before firing home. Five minutes later Jansson powered home a towering header to make it 2-2.

It appeared that would be it, a decent point, but Roofe fired home the winner in the fifth minute of stoppage time to spark incredible scenes.

It was even tighter in the next game, on Boxing Day against Blackburn. Everything seemed to be going to plan when Leeds took the lead after thirty-three minutes, but Rovers equalised two minutes into the second half. When Charlie Mulgrew gave them a lead at the death, things looked desperate, but Roofe scored twice in injury-time to secure another breathtaking 3-2 victory.

United's momentum was halted by two defeats over the following six days as Leeds demonstrated their vulnerabilities. They retained top spot, but Norwich, Sheffield United and West Bromwich Albion were closing fast.

Exit from the FA Cup at QPR was irrelevant given the second-string nature of Bielsa's selection but a chance to restore some confidence was lost.

Faith in Bielsa's leadership remained strong but United had snatched defeat from the jaws of victory on too many occasions in the past to take anything for granted – supporters refused to put any stock in the noise about teams on top at Christmas always securing promotion.

As Leeds prepared for their home game with Derby on 11 January, Bielsa despatched a member of staff to covertly observe the Rams' training session. When he was spotted and reported to the police, there was a huge furore about the ethics of the matter and a self-righteous Frank Lampard accused Bielsa of a lack of sportsmanship. There was a flurry of support for Lampard with media pundits pillorying Bielsa. 'Spygate' was a storm in a teacup, though the noise dragged on for months, with a number of Leeds' Championship rivals demanding an inquiry.

As luck would have it, Sky Sports was covering the game on a freezing Friday night. Anchorman Scott Minto described what it was like as the tension ramped up.

'The whole running order of the show was ripped up. We had done all our prep in the days before and then travelled to Leeds, and then this massive story breaks. We arrived at the ground and it all felt very different. It is a rare thing to get big, breaking news like that on the day of a game, so it was all so fresh and exciting to cover. To give credit to Bielsa, he wanted to come out and talk, and it added a huge element of importance to the show.'

Bielsa fronted up and admitted that he had indeed sent someone to spy on Derby's training session, adding that it was something he had always practiced.

'I would have thought it would have impacted more negatively upon Leeds as they were the ones being called unsportsmanlike,' added Minto, 'but it seemed to have more of an effect on Derby. Leeds, meanwhile, seemed to rise to it ... It was one of their best displays of the season, and probably one of Derby's worst. It was quite surprising.'

Leeds won 2-0 to maintain their promotion push, but the club was fined £200,000 by the EFL for the incident.

Leeds announced that Bielsa would hold an impromptu press conference later in the week, prompting some to speculate that he was going to walk away from the club. Not a bit of it, as the Argentine delivered an elaborate presentation to demonstrate that surveillance was merely the cherry on the cake of the vast preparation that he lavished on every game.

Bielsa settled the fine himself, saying, 'The sanction [the EFL] gave us of £200,000 – it is a financial sanction against the club, not against me, but I am responsible for it. That is why I paid it from my pocket, the financial sanction.'

In a trice, Bielsa had defused all the criticism and emerged with even more support than he previously enjoyed.

Klich played up to the controversy at the final whistle against Derby, putting both hands to his eyes in a 'binocular' gesture. Leeds fans loved it on Twitter and devised *Stop Crying Frank Lampard*, a mickey-take of the Oasis song *Stop Crying Your Heart Out*.

If Leeds laughed things off at the time, they were soon less happy, stumbling through the weeks that followed, losing at Stoke, winning narrowly at struggling Rotherham and losing at home to Norwich. The Canaries took top spot on goal difference as Sheffield United closed to within three points after thirty games.

The promotion battle between the three joined in earnest, with two automatic slots on offer.

After fifteen Championship starts for him, the manager decided that Samu Saiz was not a Bielsa man, sending him off on loan to Getafe in Spain on New Year's Day. The fans implored Bielsa to strengthen in the window, but all they got was a goalkeeper to replace Blackman, who had returned to parent club Chelsea after breaking his tibia.

That said, the goalkeeper was a big name. Kiko Casilla had won three Champions League medals with Real Madrid and United made him the highest-paid player at Elland Road.

It was not that Leeds hadn't pursued others. Victor Orta nearly signed Daniel James, the Swansea winger, but the Swans went cold on the deal in the closing hours of the window to leave both Orta and James beside themselves with dismay.

Leeds regained their form in February and gave a wonderful display on 1 March to hammer West Brom 4-0 at Elland Road. The victory allowed them to leapfrog Norwich and Sheffield United to regain top spot, though the Canaries won at Millwall the next day to regain their ascendancy.

United won their next two games at Bristol City and Reading without conceding but Norwich and the Blades stubbornly dogged their steps.

And next up were Sheffield United at Elland Road. Victory would give Leeds a five-point cushion over the visitors.

Unfortunately, the Whites couldn't make home advantage count and Sheffield inflicted a mortal wound, scoring the only goal of the game after seventy-one minutes. To add to the pain, Casilla was sent off in injury-time.

Leeds slipped to third but bounced back a week later to defeat Millwall while the Blades lost at home to Bristol City. Fortunes fluctuated wildly over the course of the final twenty minutes. After seventy-one minutes, Sheffield took a 2-1 lead with Leeds losing by the same score. Ayling instantly equalised for the Whites. Seventy-seven minutes and Weimann scored for

Bristol and six minutes later Hernandez won the game for Leeds just as Weimann completed his hat-trick to finish off Sheffield. It was almost more than nerves could bear.

With seven games to go, Norwich had pulled well clear at the top and Leeds had a two-point advantage over Sheffield United. Surely, Bielsa's men had enough in the tank to see out the job?

Never say such a thing to a Leeds United fan!

On 6 April, Norwich rubbed in their superiority by beating QPR 4-0, and it was suddenly advantage Sheffield United as they won at Preston while Leeds stumbled to defeat at Birmingham.

Three days later and another twist with Leeds winning 2-0 at Preston and Sheffield held to a draw at Birmingham. Five games to go and Leeds ahead by a point as the tension grew.

Sheffield United gave Leeds more encouragement when they could only draw at home to Millwall in the lunchtime kick-off on 13 April. Bielsa's men capitalised when Jack Harrison scored the only goal of the game with Sheffield Wednesday.

Three points clear of the Blades, Leeds now needed ten points from their remaining four games to confirm promotion.

Just as the finishing line came into sight, something got hold of the United players.

On 19 April they had a 'gimme' at home to relegation-threatened Wigan. They had seen Sheffield escape with a victory from a testing game at home to Nottingham Forest, but they started as if they were going to romp home against the Latics.

Things looked good after fourteen minutes when Wigan centre-back Cedric Kipre was dismissed for handling on the line. Hernandez rapped his spot kick against the post, but three minutes later Bamford latched onto a through ball and hammered home confidently.

Leeds threatened to run riot but they let Wigan back into the contest and Gavin Massey shot past Casilla to equalise just before the break. Seventeen minutes into the second half, the same player headed Wigan ahead and they withstood everything an anxious Leeds side could throw at them and secured a shock victory.

'Destiny gave us a red card, a penalty and fifteen chances to score,' said a mortified Bielsa. 'We simply should have won that game today. I am sad at this defeat, but I am very motivated. We have had a good season, but it will mean nothing if we do not get promoted … This is a very serious wound in the worst moment.'

It was a day to forget, but it was almost impossible for Leeds supporters to do so. They could almost hear the strains of 'Leeds, Leeds are falling apart – AGAIN' at rivals' stadia all across the country.

It made the trip to Brentford a must win, but Leeds' record against the Bees at Griffin Park was dismal. They had not won at the ground since August 1950 and when Sheffield United ran out easy lunchtime winners at Hull, the task became monumental.

Bielsa recalled Cooper and Forshaw in place of Berardi and Phillips and Leeds dominated the early stages with Bamford firing wide from inside the area. Leeds were furious when they were inexplicably denied a penalty after Julian Jeanvier swept Bamford's legs from under him. Referee Keith Stroud shrugged off the appeals but it was an obvious injustice.

Brentford took the lead on the stroke of half-time after Sergi Canos played Neil Maupay in on goal.

Leeds had the early chances in the second half but Canos was in inspired form and doubled Brentford's lead after sixty-two minutes, flicking the ball past Casilla. Maupay nearly made it 3-0 minutes later but skied an acrobatic effort.

The body language of Bielsa and the players told the story at the end. Hernandez left the field in tears and the coach admitted his side's automatic promotion chances looked slim. The Argentine shook every one of his players' hands at the end 'because we all saw that our possibility to finish first and second were decreasing ... and the players felt that too. I thought they deserved that for all the effort they made.'

Sheffield United virtually wrapped things up the following Saturday by beating Ipswich. They had a six-point lead and a goal difference superiority of thirteen.

It made Leeds' game on the Sunday against Aston Villa, the division's form side, a dead rubber but somehow United found the resilience to dominate. The afternoon would be remembered, however, for a controversial five-minute spell as the game moved into its final quarter.

All afternoon, Villa had infuriated the Leeds fans with their outrageous diving and when Cooper left Jonathan Kodjia sprawling with a heavy tackle, there were only cheers round Elland Road. As the ball fell to Roberts, several Villa players pulled up, expecting him to put it out to allow treatment.

Roberts passed down the line to Klich, who later claimed he hadn't seen the incident, and went on to score, provoking mayhem. The Villa players were incensed and manhandled Klich disgracefully; Bamford appeared to go down injured, claiming he had been punched and Anwar El Ghazi was shown the red card. Villa boss Dean Smith and assistant John Terry stridently confronted Bielsa and his coaching staff and matters threatened to get out of hand.

The game resumed after a stoppage of five minutes with Bielsa directing his players to allow Villa to score. Jansson was unsympathetic and attempted a tackle, but his teammates obeyed Bielsa's instructions and Albert Adomah walked in the equaliser.

Bielsa was lauded afterwards for his sportsmanship, but merely said, 'We just gave the goal back. Everyone saw the facts. We expressed our interpretation of the facts by doing what we did. English football is known for this [sportsmanship].'

Bamford was given a retrospective two-match suspension for attempting to deceive an official and El Ghazi's red card was rescinded.

Leeds lost their final game against Ipswich, but the result was irrelevant with all eyes on the lottery of the play-offs and a resumption of the season-long feud with Frank Lampard and Derby County.

It appeared that Leeds had done the hardest part of the job at Pride Park after Roofe's fifteenth goal of the season earned first-leg victory.

Derby were incensed when assistant referee Eddie Smart persuaded referee Craig Pawson to overturn his award of a penalty to the Rams with fourteen minutes to go – Harrison had been adjudged to have fouled Jayden Bogle.

The home side also felt Klich should have been dismissed for a butt to Fikayo Tomori's chest as he rose to his feet after going down under a challenge. He was given a yellow card over the incident.

The match served merely as an appetiser for the game of the season as Bielsa and Lampard locked horns again at Elland Road on 15 May.

It was an emotion-filled evening at Elland Road with the Leeds fans in fine voice. Bamford returned to replace the injured Roofe while Bielsa left the fit-again Jansson on the bench.

It was a feisty encounter from the first whistle – Leeds fans took a particular dislike to Derby captain Richard Keogh who threw his considerable bulk about without incurring the wrath of referee Anthony Taylor.

Leeds were on the front foot early doors and after twenty-four minutes, Dallas pounced when Cooper's header came back off the post. He slammed the ball home to give his side a two-goal aggregate lead. The roar echoed into the night sky as Leeds took a massive step towards the Wembley final.

They were playing well if not quite at their best, but Lampard shook things up, bringing Jack Marriott off the bench a minute before the break. He had an instant impact and when Casilla came racing out to deal with a situation that Cooper seemed to have under control, the two Leeds men got in each other's way and the ball ran clear for Marriott to poke home.

Leeds came out after the break ready to snatch back the momentum but they never got the chance. A minute in, Chelsea loanee Mason Mount put Derby ahead on the night.

Just before the hour, Cooper was adjudged to have pulled Mason Bennett's shirt in the area and the referee awarded Derby a penalty. Liverpool loanee Harry Wilson made no mistake from the spot and suddenly the Rams were ahead.

Within four minutes, the aggregate scores were level when Dallas scored his second, cutting in from the left to fire home spectacularly.

Such moments often spark a fightback and certainly Leeds had the best of the next ten, but they lost their way when Berardi was sent off after seventy-eight minutes for retaliating after several heavy challenges. Seven minutes later and Marriott poked Derby ahead.

Rams defender Scott Malone was dismissed for a second yellow in injury-time, but Leeds were beaten, sentenced to a tenth successive season in the Championship.

Tears were shed all around Elland Road and Bielsa summed up a sad evening afterwards.

'It's a painful situation and I'm disappointed. We should have had one or two more in the first half and then the second half broke immediately. We lost control. We had twenty minutes without control and I couldn't find a solution.'

His voice trailed away wistfully as he gazed into the far distance. On that devastating evening, no one knew whether Marcelo Bielsa would be back to try again.

CHAPTER TWENTY-TWO

We Go Again

The summer of 2019 could have seen Bielsa walk away from Elland Road. The longest he had ever stayed at a club side was two years with Athletic Bilbao – his time at Lazio was a mere forty-eight hours. However, this was an honourable man, determined to finish the job he had started for people he liked. He had formed a powerful bond with the city of Leeds, the players and the supporters and he answered in the affirmative when the moment came.

Bielsa would lead another promotion challenge, to the enormous relief of Radrizzani and everyone connected with Leeds United.

The terms of his contract were never an issue for Bielsa; all he sought was reassurances over his ambitions for the squad.

Bielsa understood the realities of the EFL's profit and sustainability rules only too well. That much had been apparent twelve months earlier when he agreed to the sale of Vieira in order to fund the purchase of Bamford.

The nine-point sanction applied by the EFL to Birmingham City for financial transgressions brought the issue home to many in the Championship and Bielsa accepted the need for prudent trading.

What was important to him was how the balance was struck. Some players would be retained at any cost, with the obvious example being Kalvin Phillips. A number of Bielsa's managerial postings had run aground on the rocks of transfer policy after Bielsa was not allowed control of player comings and goings.

His departure from Lazio came after it became clear the club would not pursue his preferred transfer targets. Similarly, he quit Marseille in France after just one season because of broken promises at boardroom level.

Radrizzani and Victor Orta were fully aware of such issues and would not think of doing anything to offend Bielsa. The coach sported a satisfied smile when both United and Phillips rejected the overtures from promoted

Aston Villa despite the £25 million on offer. Leeds United under Radrizzani was a very different enterprise from the selling club of the previous decade and a half.

Now, the only ones to depart were those whom Bielsa regarded as replaceable or problematic or where the player himself wanted to move on.

Bailey Peacock-Farrell was in the first group, let go to Burnley. Nineteen-year-old Illan Meslier was recruited on loan from Lorient of France as backup to first-choice Kiko Casilla.

Jack Clarke, also considered dispensable, was shipped out to Tottenham for a fee in the region of £11 million. He would still be available on a season-long loan, as was marquee signing Helder Costa from Wolves, while Manchester City's Jack Harrison returned for a second loan spell.

Samu Saiz had been allocated to the problematic category the previous Christmas and sent out on loan. His exit was made permanent with a £2.5 million move to Girona.

It had become obvious that there was tension in Bielsa's relationship with Pontus Jansson which went far beyond the Swede's refusal to allow Aston Villa free passage to score in April. The supporters were less than convinced but Bielsa had no doubts about releasing Jansson to Brentford. All the concerns were allayed by the performances of Brighton loanee Ben White, an impeccable and cool defender who perfectly fitted Bielsa's requirement for a ball-playing centre-back.

Top scorer Kemar Roofe made it evident that he wanted a move when Leeds confirmed they would not match Bamford's wage. He joined Anderlecht for £7 million. Again, Bielsa got a decent replacement in Arsenal's young goal poacher Eddie Nketiah.

The total sum raised was a whisker short of £30 million and chief executive Angus Kinnear pronounced himself well pleased with the summer's trading.

Bielsa expressed doubts publicly over whether he could rouse the players to another year of performances beyond their normal level and certainly there were anxieties among the fans.

Within thirty minutes of the first whistle of the first game, all such apprehension was cast to the four winds. Away to Bristol City, White offered clear evidence that he was no second-rate Jansson substitute with his cool head and exceptional skill. Hernandez also started in splendid fashion, settling any nerves with a sublimely swerved opening goal. The Spaniard laid on another score for Bamford and Harrison added a third before Andreas Weimann netted a consolation for City.

The season rose and fell with the fortunes and performances of Hernandez. When El Mago was on song, threading his killer passes through the eye of a needle, or finding the net with a masterful finish, then Leeds rolled like a smooth and powerful juggernaut, devouring everything in its way. When the

Wizard was absent or drifted out of a game, as he sometimes did, then Leeds laboured, devoid of inspiration.

The spot kick Hernandez missed against Wigan in April had knocked his confidence and his influence diminished. He had an anonymous game in the play-off showdown with Derby, one of the key reasons that the Rams seized control of midfield.

'I think in the difficult moments of the games the players need to take responsibility,' said Hernandez. 'I think in some moments I need to take this responsibility because I have experience. I try to show my teammates even in the bad moments that we need everybody.'

'He's a real silent leader,' said Bielsa.

With Hernandez in place, Leeds took sixteen points from the first seven games. They were on course for another victory in their eighth game, leading Derby by a goal at Elland Road on 21 September when Bielsa withdrew a limping Hernandez. The Rams snatched an injury-time equaliser.

He missed the next six games, only two of which Leeds won. Each was notable, a vital but narrow win against major promotion rivals West Bromwich Albion and the game against Birmingham at Elland Road on 19 October, which topped off a week of celebrations as the club commemorated the centenary of its formation. The team wore a special kit devoid of any sponsorship and pre-game there was a parade of former players.

The football didn't match the occasion and Leeds found it difficult to break down a determined Birmingham rearguard. Phillips scored the only goal after sixty-five minutes, sliding in on Harrison's square pass to beat goalkeeper Lee Camp. The three points saw Leeds climb into second behind West Bromwich Albion.

Leeds were up and running, intent on making no mistakes this time around. The team was playing much more coherent and assured football than a year earlier. Certainly, they were stronger defensively with Cooper and White forming an excellent partnership. United's domination of possession was outstanding but their conversion rate was a worry. Bamford had started the season with a flurry of goals but was now struggling to take chances. The hatful of opportunities he passed up at Charlton condemned Leeds to defeat by a messy goal and his brittle confidence gave way.

Happily, Nketiah's cameo appearances demonstrated his quality as a poacher and others regularly chipped in. The fans implored Bielsa to play Bamford and Nketiah as a partnership, but he ignored the pleas, committed to a lone striker with a five-man midfield to satisfy his obsession with dominating the middle of the field.

They stumbled to draws in the two away games that followed but then regained their mojo with seven wins in a row, five of them with clean sheets. It was no coincidence that the victories returned with Hernandez.

On 2 November, they were leading QPR by a single goal from Tyler Roberts and struggling to finish things off. Hernandez came on for Helder Costa and within five minutes, Jack Harrison notched a second to secure victory.

The 4-0 hammering of Middlesbrough on 30 November caught Leeds at their imperious best, a reinvigorated Bamford opening the scoring with his third goal in four games.

Victory against Hull on 10 December left Leeds topping the table with an eleven-point cushion over third-placed Fulham. They seemed set fair for the promotion they had pursued for so long.

Events over the following two months called such hopes into question.

All appeared right with the world when Leeds stormed to a three-goal lead within fifty-two minutes against Cardiff, but they were found wanting as the Welsh side fought back. They had to be content with a point from a 3-3 draw that in the circumstances felt more like a defeat.

Leeds lost 2-1 at promotion rivals Fulham a week later and then dropped a point at home to Preston. Suddenly, anxieties were all-consuming. Nerves were tested to the limit on 29 December in a breathtaking game at Birmingham.

With Bamford absent with a dead leg, Bielsa gave Nketiah a rare start. Things seemed to be working when Leeds took a two-goal lead inside twenty minutes. Birmingham were redoubtable opposition, however, and pulled one back before the half-hour. Leeds didn't take the lesson to heart and Jutkiewicz equalised just after the hour. Inside the next ten minutes, Leeds came storming back to restore their lead with a wonderful strike from Ayling. That should have been enough, but Bela nodded in from a free kick in the eighty-third minute for 3-3. Dallas scooped in a fourth for Leeds within sixty seconds but again Jutkiewicz equalised, sliding in a fourth in injury-time.

Incredibly, things were not yet done. In the fifth minute of stoppage time, a marauding Ayling fired a ball across Birmingham's 6-yard box. Caught in the headlights, Wes Harding sliced the ball into his own net. 5-4 in one of the most talked about games of the season.

With Albion losing to Middlesbrough, Leeds were suddenly back at the top of the table.

A New Year's Day draw at West Brom did nothing to undermine the promotion claims of either side and left Leeds with a nine-point lead on Brentford in third.

It was now, however, that the problems really began with a run of three points from five games. The spell culminated in a disastrous defeat at Nottingham Forest with Leeds' promotion cushion all but gone and Brentford, Fulham and Forest breathing down their necks.

Enough was enough and Bielsa took command of the situation, sitting the players down and giving them an inspirational talking to, objectively laying out the reality of their situation. Their play was as good as ever, he insisted, the failures down to fine margins. They were still creating chances and dominating possession. All that was needed to restore the natural order was converting their opportunities.

Barely a month previously, Leeds had impressed a television audience with an outstanding display at Arsenal in the FA Cup. They showed exactly what a good side they were, outplaying the Gunners in the first half. They could not take their chances and ended up losing to a single goal, but the performance offered ample evidence for Bielsa's rallying call.

Bielsa's post-Forest pep talk became part of Leeds folklore, shaking the squad out of its anxiety and dragging the players back to the matter in hand. The impact was telling.

There was one player, however, for whom there was no redemption.

Kiko Casilla had been in poor form, spreading anxiety across his back four with his eccentricity and impulsive rushes from his line. His error at his near post prompted the disaster at Forest. Doubtless, accusations of racism going back to September were clouding his mind.

Charlton player Jonathan Leko had accused the Spaniard of racially abusing him and the Football Association had been considering the case for months. A verdict was not expected until the end of February.

The game at Brentford on 11 February was massive – the Bees knew victory could see them leapfrog Leeds with Fulham and Forest on the verge of doing likewise.

The evening was disastrous for Casilla – he misjudged Cooper's back pass, allowed the ball to run under his foot and stumbled as he attempted to recover. Said Benrahma capitalised, racing in to touch the ball home.

Leeds could have been forgiven for falling apart at that point, but they dragged themselves into the game. They quickly equalised when Cooper powered home after Brentford failed to clear a corner and dominated the contest.

They couldn't convert the point into three, but the slide had been arrested. When Fulham and Forest both dropped points later in the week, Leeds' second position was still intact, albeit on goal difference alone. A corner had been turned and confidence restored by a resilient performance.

Leeds capitalised with two 1-0 victories, both at Elland Road, over Bristol City and Reading. Just as important, they returned their first clean sheets since mid-December and the points gap to Fulham was stretched to five.

Relegation-threatened Middlesbrough should have been easy meat at the Riverside, but Leeds laboured to a third successive single-goal win. At a time like this, points not performances were the thing.

The result was immediately forgotten when the news came through that the FA had found Casilla guilty of racism. They banned him for eight games with a fine of £60,000. He would miss almost the entirety of United's run-in. He was devastated.

That gave an opportunity for young Frenchman Illan Meslier to show what he could do. He had performed admirably when he made his first-team debut in the Cup at Arsenal and United supporters were almost uniformly relieved at Casilla's enforced absence, convinced by Meslier's potential.

He had an easy time of things in his first game, with Leeds winning 4-0 at Hull, the rout launched by a spectacular strike from an airborne Luke Ayling after just five minutes. The right-back was enjoying a purple patch, giving a succession of outstanding displays on his way to becoming the EFL Championship PFA Player of the Year.

Hernandez made it two at the start of the second half and Roberts came off the bench to grab a brace in the last ten minutes.

Ayling was at it again a week later when he opened the scoring against Huddersfield inside three minutes. Bamford increased the advantage at the start of the second half.

Leeds had won five games on the bounce with not a goal conceded. With nine matches left, they topped the table for the first time since December and increased the gap to third-placed Fulham to seven points. Surely the supporters could finally start to celebrate a return to the big time.

But unforeseen events 5,000 miles away on the other side of the world were about to change the shape of the season, indeed the history of the entire globe.

The Covid-19 pandemic was the world's first since SARS in 2003 and the worst since the Spanish Flu of 1918.

It took a while before the scale of the disease became apparent but in mid-March, it was confirmed that all Premier League and EFL football was suspended, initially for a month. In the event, it was 17 June before fixtures restarted.

There had been fears that the EFL would declare the season null and void, which would have been soul-destroying for Leeds, but such drastic action was avoided. All games would be played but they would take place behind closed doors with no spectators as a safety precaution, a dire outcome for a club with such loyal support.

United's first game after the resumption was at Cardiff on 21 June. Bielsa had got Leeds back at peak fitness after their break and they appeared ready to see off the Bluebirds with little trouble.

Phillips had a lapse of concentration after thirty-five minutes, his loose pass falling straight to Junior Hoilett, who advanced on an exposed back four before firing home from outside the penalty area. After seventy-one minutes, there was almost a carbon copy with Cooper the guilty party. Robert Glatzel had the time and space to pick his spot and find the net off the inside of the post.

'We could have won, we should have won,' complained Bielsa. 'We created enough chances to score the necessary goals. They needed our mistakes to score, but we know we should have been clearer to finish the attacks. We lacked something in the match in the final third … We have eight matches left and we cannot think everything is set.'

It was eerie playing in front of a deserted stadium. 'You cannot replace supporters,' said Bielsa. 'What I wish is football, the business of football, doesn't discover they can play without fans.'

Fulham in third were the visitors to Elland Road six days later and had the better of the first half, despite Bamford giving Leeds the lead after ten minutes. United came good in the second half with Alioski and Harrison scoring to wrap up an emphatic 3-0 victory.

With West Brom losing at home to Brentford, Leeds were three points clear at the top and eight ahead of the Bees, who had emerged as the main danger to the top two.

Leeds struggled to see off second bottom Luton on 30 June and fell behind to a Harry Cornick goal after fifty minutes. The ever-reliable Dallas netted an equaliser thirteen minutes later. Despite having 75 per cent of the possession, Leeds could not force a second.

They held their nerve to win 3-1 at Blackburn four days later, settled by a seventh-minute goal from Bamford. Phillips curled home a gorgeous second from a free kick just before half-time, but Adam Armstrong pulled one back from an even better dead ball strike three minutes into the second half. Anxieties were eased within five minutes when Klich netted a third.

The result gave Leeds a four-point advantage on West Bromwich Albion and six on Brentford. The Whites seemed to be holding their nerve better than anyone although the late surge by Brentford had everyone rattled.

It took a while for Leeds to find a way through Stoke City's massed defence at Elland Road on 9 July, but Klich coolly slotted away a penalty on the stroke of half-time following a foul on Costa. The second half was a procession after Costa added a second two minutes in and Leeds looked assured – they coasted to a 5-0 victory that left them needing seven points from four games to make promotion absolutely certain.

In the circumstances, a point from the fixture at Swansea on 12 July would have been good enough. Leeds looked like they were playing for the clean sheet, content for the most part to contain the home side. But up popped Hernandez with the winner a minute from time to spark exuberant celebrations.

Two days later, Fulham's draw at West Brom offered further assurance, with the Londoners no longer able to catch Leeds. Four points from three games was now the requirement.

Leeds were next in action on Thursday 16 July at home to relegation-threatened Barnsley. At such a stage of any season, games like this were always a potential banana skin and no one at Elland Road was taking anything for granted.

The Tykes pushed Leeds all the way and Bielsa spent most of the afternoon tweaking to cope with Barnsley's smart football. However, Leeds got the win they just about deserved when Michael Sollbauer put the ball into his own net after twenty-eight minutes as he tried to clear a drilled cross from Bamford.

Two games to go and one point required, Leeds could start dreaming.

As it turned out, they didn't even need the point. The following day, West Brom came unstuck, losing to a late goal at Huddersfield and Leeds' promotion was confirmed. It was a riotous evening around the stadium with fans and players celebrating the dream they had pursued for so many years.

LEEDS WERE UP!

They were crowned champions the following day when Stoke City beat Brentford.

It was perhaps understandable that Sunday's game against Derby at Pride Park was a low-key affair, Leeds only starting to play after falling behind to a Chris Martin goal after fifty-four minutes. They were sufficiently insulted to carve out three goals to secure victory and revenge for the play-off agony a year earlier.

Liam Cooper was presented with the Championship trophy following a 4-0 thrashing of Charlton. Leeds' football was sleek and irresistible, a gala display with Ben White starting the fun with a wonderful strike from the edge of the area. There were cheers for Marcelo Bielsa as he humbly participated in the celebrations, wildly cheered as he raised the trophy with a huge grin lighting up his face.

Leeds were the worthiest of champions, ending the season a full ten points clear of West Brom. United had delivered six straight victories as their rivals buckled under the pressure of the chase.

It was a proud moment to be a fan of Leeds United.

CHAPTER TWENTY-THREE
The Stubborn Idealist

'Foolhardy, stubborn, naïve,' said his critics.

'Principled, uncompromising, genius,' said his disciples.

'Dull, boring, pragmatic,' said no one.

Was there anyone associated with the Premier League in 2020 who divided opinion quite as sharply as Marcelo Bielsa? You would be hard pressed to find them.

And the outcomes for Leeds United fluctuated just as wildly in their haphazard journey through their first year back in the big time. There were hammerings from Manchester United, Leicester, Crystal Palace and Tottenham and breathtaking victories against Aston Villa, Newcastle and West Brom; depressing days against Crawley, Brighton, West Ham and Wolves and uplifting afternoons against Liverpool, Man City, Fulham and Everton.

They certainly didn't hold back, right from the moment Andrea Radrizzani stumped up £96 million for Victor Orta to play with. In came Rodrigo, Robin Koch, Diego Llorente and Raphinha, but still the Championship spine held sway, Cooper, Ayling, Phillips and Dallas, while Patrick Bamford convinced people he could make it in the Premier League after all.

Rarely this last twenty years has a promoted team taken such scant heed of reputation. And the world loved them for it, loved them and pitied them in equal measure. Shoddy at set pieces yet bossing possession, Leeds United were a force of nature as they breezed through their return to the Premier League, as likely to make you cry as leave you laughing.

It made a nonsense of Radrizzani's stated desire for a year of consolidation, securing their future in the top flight, but few were complaining, including the United owner.

Any other team visiting Anfield, home of champions Liverpool, on the opening day would have been circumspect, played with caution and with a defensive mindset, but that was out of the question for Bielsa and Leeds.

They played without their captain, Liam Cooper, waylaid by injury on Scotland duty and the new centre-back pairing of Pascal Struijk and Koch struggled to cope with Mo Salah, conceding two penalties and allowing the Egyptian superstar to kick off with a hat-trick. They didn't despair, hitting back with thrilling strikes from Harrison, Bamford and Klich. A more pragmatic team might have held out for the point that seemed to be coming their way for much of the second half, but that was not Bielsa's way and he was applauded for the way he set about the champions, notwithstanding the 4-3 defeat.

Victories against Fulham and Sheffield United offered reassurance that Leeds meant business and three goals in three games established Bamford's Premier League credentials. He snatched an extraordinary hat-trick as Leeds won 3-0 at Villa on 23 October, but the victory was sandwiched by dispiriting defeats to Wolves, Leicester and Palace as the reality of top-fight football hit home.

Leeds bounced back at home to Arsenal, but had to be content with a goalless draw, struggling to break through against ten men after Nicolas Pepe was dismissed for a butt on Alioski. They should have won the game and a goal from Raphinha saw to it that they came away with all three points from a trip to Goodison to face Everton.

If Leeds thought they had turned a corner, they had a rude shock as Chelsea and West Ham inflicted comprehensive defeats. A 5-2 hammering of Newcastle captured Leeds at their most impressive in front of goal, but their defensive vulnerability was badly exposed when Manchester United ran in six at Old Trafford.

Criticism of Bielsa intensified after that game with many pundits slating him for a naïve refusal to compromise his natural desire for attack at all costs. Bielsa took his critics to task in a defiant press conference and then proved his point with clean sheet victories against Burnley and West Brom, the latter a five-goal rout of Sam Allardyce's men at the Hawthorns.

The first three games of 2021 suggested that Leeds had hit a brick wall. They lost 3-0 at Tottenham, collapsed at Crawley in the FA Cup and then lost at home to Brighton. A post-Christmas malaise was nothing new for Leeds: the first seven games of 2020 yielded a single victory; in 2018/19 there were four defeats in the six games after Boxing Day; a year earlier was even worse, eight points and one win from the fourteen following Boxing Day.

At such a crucial time of their first campaign back in the Premier League, it was essential that Leeds didn't go into freefall. The trip to Newcastle on 26 January was massive, especially as the struggling Magpies were only four points below United. The Whites came up with the goods with goals from Raphinha and Harrison earning the three points. Days later they did even better, hammering Leicester 3-1 with Bamford earning rave reviews for an all-round display that suggested he might be ripe for an England call.

With Rodrigo and Raphinha both taken off with injuries before the end, Leeds finished with what amounted to their Championship side, shoving their critics' words down their throats. Bielsa was continuing to get extraordinary performances out of players who had been mid-table nobodies in the Championship before he got hold of them.

Leeds' patchy accumulation of points was sufficient to keep them bobbing along in a comfortable mid-table spot, but they came unstuck against Everton when they played their first game on newly laid turf purchased from Tottenham. The pandemic put paid to a plan to relay the turf the previous summer, but the club had to do something about the ploughed field nature of the playing surface.

The new turf was not the answer with players slipping all over the place and Everton taking a two-goal lead in the first half. Pascal Struijk was badly at fault for the first goal, playing Digne onside and reacting too slowly to cut out the cross. Leeds came storming back after the break and should have won but were denied by an outstanding display from Everton reserve keeper Robin Olsen.

Leeds rose to the occasion once more when they comprehensively beat Crystal Palace and returned to the top half of the table as a result. The score was only 2-0 but it was a comprehensive performance from Leeds at their best.

Four goals were conceded without reply by a minute into the second half of the Valentine's Day game at Arsenal with Illan Meslier having a nightmare. Leeds, seemingly unconcerned, upped their game and the Gunners were praying for the final whistle when Struijk and Costa pulled back two goals and Leeds suggested they might go further. In the end, they couldn't and the headlines were all about the return to form of hat-trick hero Pierre-Emerick Aubameyang, though the never-say-die attacking spirit demanded by Bielsa continued to impress.

Meslier was also the villain when Leeds lost narrowly at Wolves, unlucky to concede an own goal when Adama Traore's driven shot bounced down off the bar and went in off the back of the keeper's head.

With Leeds still eight shy of the forty-point figure generally considered the safety bar, there were still some nerves at Elland Road, even if everyone else confidently predicted, 'There's no way that Leeds are going down.' We'd heard the old cliché about being too good to go down almost twenty years previously, so United fans wouldn't count their chickens until they were certain of survival. The players gave them some more assurance when they blitzed an out-of-form Southampton 3-0, goals from Bamford, Dallas and Raphinha quickly ending the match as a contest. 'Football on steroids' was the very apt description.

An unlucky single-goal defeat at home to Aston Villa and failure at West Ham showed that Leeds were still not yet ready to launch a push for the upper echelons of the league, though they competed manfully to earn a goalless draw against high-flying Chelsea, unbeaten under Thomas Tuchel.

Leeds had yet to win a game in the capital under Bielsa and talk of the London Curse made the trip to Fulham appear a challenge, but United proved themselves a class above the Cottagers, winning more easily than the 2-1 score suggested. With the Londoners the team most likely to escape of the three in the relegation zone, the victory was crucial, opening Leeds' advantage over them to thirteen points as they moved on to thirty-nine. It meant that the fans were finally able to start banking on a second season in the Premier League as the season entered the international break.

When they returned to action, the Whites laboured at home to rock bottom Sheffield United but took the three points that finally saw them reach the forty-point mark with eight games to spare. And breathe!

Bielsa's stay at Leeds bypassed the 1,000-day milestone on 11 March and he seemed to be loving the job as much as he had when he first arrived. However, his customary unwillingness to discuss a renewal of his contract until the season was over set the more jaundiced members of the press spinning away on unwarranted claims that a parting of the ways was coming. The rumours intensified when stories emerged that Leeds were laying contingencies in case the worst came to the worst.

It was just sound planning, of course, but it made us start to wonder whether there was any truth to the story. Bielsa's actions thus far indicated not but fans brought up on expecting the worst were shaken to the core with anxiety – this was simply too glorious a relationship to end.

CHAPTER TWENTY-FOUR

Bye Bye Big Six

The final few months of the 2020/21 season eloquently reminded everybody of the all-pervading influence of money on Premier League football.

Leeds United's accounts for the year to July 2020 revealed the full costs of achieving promotion and the unpalatable implications of failing to do so.

The club had made a profit only once in the previous eight years – £1 million in 2016/17 – and losses had increased significantly under Radrizzani's leadership, widening now from £21 million to £62 million, despite revenue climbing from £49 million to £54 million. Expenditure included £20 million in promotion bonuses and a rebate of £7 million to broadcasters.

The consequences of a failure to win promotion were almost unthinkable. Promotion bonuses would have been avoided and the costs of Covid-19 were deductible, but Leeds could well have faced a points sanction.

There was some speculation that the scale of the deficit hinted at an ongoing problem but the extra TV money on offer in the Premier League and the significant position-based bonuses would comfortably offset expenditure. Even the lack of gate money could not dampen the feel-good factor. Eleventh place in the Premier League would be worth around £120 million based on 2018/19's distribution.

Missing out on promotion could have spelled the break-up of Bielsa's squad to avoid a Financial Fair Play breach.

Fulham's defeat at home to Wolves on a Friday night in early April all but guaranteed United's Premier League future. It was just as well with upcoming fixtures against Liverpool and the two Manchester clubs. Few supporters seriously anticipated any points from that run.

The game with Manchester City saw a mutual love-in between Bielsa and City coach Pep Guardiola.

'He's a magical man,' Bielsa said of Guardiola. 'What he knows how to do is extremely difficult for me to try [to copy] and I've already given up, but I have genuine admiration for what he does. Interpreting the novel decisions that he incorporates into a game is already a way of falling in love with football.'

'I'm overwhelmed, I feel weird,' said Guardiola, a long-time admirer of the Argentine. 'He's the most honest person. I'm pretty sure what he says is what he believes. He doesn't say or do anything for the media for the reputation of himself. That's why I'm overwhelmed. Everyone knows the admiration and respect that I have for him and the way that he helped me from the beginning. He will always be there in my heart. If there's one person who can search or find the secrets, the way we want to play, it's him, through his work ethic and especially his knowledge about the game.'

All the pre-match talk was of City and their need for just eleven points to sew up the Premier League but then from absolutely nowhere came the result of this and many other seasons.

It was heart-warming to see Bielsa's men see off such illustrious opponents and their backs-to-the-wall resistance was all the more outstanding given the first-half dismissal of Liam Cooper.

Leeds had started reasonably although City were a street ahead of them – but then came the first-half breakthrough with Dallas finishing a decent move three minutes before half-time.

There was still time for Cooper to be dismissed for a tackle on Gabriel Jesus after a VAR review. There were doubts in the United fans' minds that it was even a foul, despite the robustness of Cooper's challenge. 'Embarrassing' was Jermaine Beckford's description in the Sky studio.

Holding City out with ten men was always going to be a big ask though Leeds fought manfully to deny them opportunities.

With fourteen minutes remaining Ferran Torres equalised and the fans feared the worst.

But Leeds started to show some forward threat of their own and as the game entered injury-time Dallas broke and slid home his second through the keeper's legs.

There were some anxious moments to come, but Leeds saw out seven minutes of added time to secure the most memorable of results.

The build-up to the game with reigning champions Liverpool was overshadowed when the news broke over the weekend of the creation of the European Super League. It was confirmed that the Anfield side, the two Manchester clubs, Chelsea, Arsenal and Tottenham had all committed to become founder members of the new league, alongside AC Milan, Atletico Madrid, Barcelona, Inter Milan, Juventus and Real Madrid. There was widespread condemnation from everybody involved in football, including managers and players from the relevant clubs. Indeed, it appeared only the owners of the Super Greedy Six had a good word to say about the initiative, although they refused to issue any comment.

The issue that united the new tournament's opponents was the removal of competition with fifteen founding members being safe from demotion and able to enjoy a monopoly. The naked avarice of the businesses that now ran football sparked an outcry, with irate Sky pundit and former Manchester United full-back Gary Neville the most vocal and eloquent, pillorying his own club and Liverpool.

Neville said he was appalled by the developments. 'I am a Manchester United fan and have been for forty years but I am disgusted, absolutely disgusted. It is an absolute disgrace. Honestly, we have to wrestle back power in this country from the clubs at the top of this league, and that includes my club.

'The motivation is greed. Deduct them all points tomorrow, put them at the bottom of the league and take the money off them. Seriously, you have got to stamp on this. It is criminal. It is a criminal act against football fans in this country. Deduct points, deduct money and punish them.

'Enough is enough. There isn't a football fan in this country that won't be seething listening to this conversation and these announcements. This is disowning-your-own-club stuff, this.

'Let them break away but punish them straight away. If they announce a letter of intent has been signed, those six clubs, they should be punished heavily. Massive fines, points deductions, take the titles off them. Give the title to Burnley, let Fulham stay up. Relegate Man United, Liverpool and Arsenal. Those three clubs, with their history in this country, are the ones that should suffer the most. The history and traditions that run through those three clubs is absolutely enormous and I value it, but they leave a lot to be desired at this moment in time.'

Leeds owner Andrea Radrizzani responded on social media, by tweeting, 'Well said Gary.'

Neville decried the timing as crass, coming amid a pandemic and just ahead of an anticipated announcement from UEFA detailing changes to the format of the Champions League.

'Seriously, in the midst of a pandemic, an economic crisis, football clubs at National League level going bust, furloughing players, clubs on the edge in League One and Two, and this lot are having Zoom calls about breaking away and basically creating more greed? Joke.

'I'd like to think Manchester United and Liverpool would stand there in the face of this and say something is not right here.

'Let's collaborate with the game to try to get a better competition, a better Champions League. I'm not against the modernisation of competitions but this is a grab. The timing is hideous. What world are these people living in to think they can bring this forward at this moment in time?'

Before the game, United players warmed up in specially made T-shirts which proclaimed, 'Earn it on the pitch, football is for the fans.' A set of shirts was left in the Liverpool dressing room but they refused to wear them, manager Jurgen Klopp spikily commenting, 'We are employees of the club and I feel responsible for a lot of things in this club. When I am involved in things then I take the criticism easily, when the boys are involved they have to take it and do that as well. But we aren't involved in this one.' He declared himself opposed to the Super League but spent most of his evening reacting to the comments of others.

Marcelo Bielsa offered a simple 'One of the reasons football is the most popular sport in the world is because the weak can beat the powerful.'

The game started with many neutrals hoping that Leeds would win, seizing the first opportunity to put one of the Big Six in their place, but when the football actually began, Liverpool bossed the first half, taking the lead through Sadio Mane. Leeds stridently fought back after the break, equalising in the closing minutes with Diego Llorente heading his first goal for the club.

The point formalised United's safety from relegation but the fact was ignored after the game as pundits continued to rail against the Super League, former Liverpool defender Jamie Carragher joining Neville to vent his spleen.

Within thirty-six hours, after vehement protests from fans around the country, all six clubs confirmed they were pulling out of the new tournament, apologising for their mistake. Their apparent remorse was transparently calculated to help them avoid sanctions and appease supporters. The announcement prompted Radrizzani to mockingly tweet 'The One-Day League?'

At the end of the week, Leeds completed their trio of games against the Big Six, playing out a dull-as-dishwater goalless draw against Manchester United. It proved conclusively how much they had improved defensively since December's thrashing at Old Trafford as they maintained their placing of ninth. Struijk and Llorente continued to flourish as a defensive partnership in Liam Cooper's absence and Kalvin Phillips masterly blotted Bruno Fernandes out of the game.

Injury was to keep the masterly Phillips out of the next game at Brighton, along with Raphinha, still suffering from the after-effects of a crude foul by Manchester City's Fernandinho in the closing minutes of Leeds' win at the Etihad.

The absence of such two telling talents debilitated Leeds as they sought to extend their unbeaten run away to Brighton – the Sussex club completed the double over a United side that was heavily criticised afterwards. Bielsa was slated for his selection and bizarre substitutions, but all was right with the world a week later when an unchanged starting eleven blitzed Tottenham at Elland Road. Novice Spurs manager Ryan Mason pointed to two Harry Kane goals disallowed for offside and another strike against the crossbar by the England captain, but the reality was stark for objective observers – Leeds had outplayed the visitors and put another of the Super Greedy Six firmly back in their place.

The passion, energy and verve of the Leeds team contrasted sharply with the lack of commitment shown by Tottenham – the game simply passed the overrated Gareth Bale by as Alioski blotted him out. The North Macedonian had been slated for a poor display at Brighton and many had expected him to be dropped with rumours abounding that he would quit Elland Road at the end of the season and throw his lot in with the hated Galatasaray. But he showed against Tottenham exactly how good he could be, condemning Bale to the shadows with a vivacious display of non-stop running.

United's 3-1 victory was more convincing than the scoreline suggested – the reality was that they had been a class above poor opponents. Raphinha marked a cameo substitute appearance by creating a wonderful opportunity for Rodrigo to lash home – the Brazilian emphasised his outstanding capabilities in his brief time on the park.

The victory completed an unbeaten home record for Leeds against the Super Greedy Six as they cemented their place in the top half of the table.

They were even better a week later, hammering Burnley 4-0 at Turf Moor. With Raphinha and Phillips restored to the starting eleven, Leeds were at their best after a slow start. Klich opened the scoring with an exquisite curler just before half-time and Harrison back-heeled home a shot from Alioski before a masterclass in finishing from Rodrigo. After coming on to replace an out-of-touch Bamford, the Spaniard showed what he could do with the right service – he scored twice, on both occasions showing excellent footwork to evade defenders and keeper before adroitly netting. For the first, he transformed Harrison's pinpoint through ball into a masterpiece, deftly evading Burnley's centre-backs with a lovely take before dinking the ball in. It was another Harrison pass that made the second, Rodrigo rounding Bailey Peacock-Farrell before side-footing home from the angle.

Burnley didn't take the defeat well, Dwight McNeil objecting violently when he thought Alioski was faking injury – the North Macedonian reacted with a mocking facial gesture which provoked an official complaint to the FA and dark accusations of racism, although it was real storm-in-a-teacup stuff.

A performance at Southampton that was sound rather than spectacular brought the tenth away victory of the season, with Leeds becoming only the second promoted team to do so in the Premier League and the first since Nottingham Forest in 1994/95. The result guaranteed that Leeds would finish in the top half of the table.

In the days that followed, fans' favourites Pablo Hernandez and Gaetano Berardi announced that they would be leaving Elland Road at the end of the season. Hernandez had three times won the supporters' vote as Player of the Year in five productive seasons at the club – Berardi was the club's longest-serving professional, joining in the madcap early weeks of Massimo Cellino's ill-starred first campaign. Berardi made his Premier League debut as a second half substitute for Diego Llorente at Southampton and Marcelo Bielsa let his heart rule his head, giving both men a start in the final game at home to West Brom.

The 8,000 supporters allowed into Elland Road gave both men a wonderful reception, willing Hernandez to top things off with a goal. He couldn't quite manage it, but he was everywhere and reminded the crowd why they adored him so much. Goals from Rodrigo, Phillips and Bamford ensured Leeds took the three points. A mistake by Kalvin Phillips in the closing minutes allowed the visitors a consolation goal and took the shine off things, but the crowd gave their heroes a rousing send-off.

The end-of-season run put to the lie for ever the myth of Bielsa Burnout and perfectly topped off United's astonishing return to the Premier League. Critics had long claimed the Argentine's intense football led to players fading in the closing weeks, but they had to eat their words – Leeds were the form team with one defeat in eleven games and ended the season with a run of four victories to climb to ninth.

The news began to break after the game that Bielsa had committed himself to Leeds for a further twelve months, much to the relief of supporters. The coach, by now almost a deity in West Yorkshire, had never revealed a shred of doubt or wavered in his commitment to attacking principles and the United fans revelled in their new environment. Despondent at being unable to witness the football in person until that final glorious afternoon, they were nevertheless warmed by United's refusal to bow to reputation. You could feel them glowing with pride at how far the team had come.

Cellino, Bates and GFH had long since been consigned to history, ghouls of Christmas Past, as the leadership of Radrizzani and Bielsa offered the promise of a glorious future.

All Leeds, aren't we?

Bibliography

Chapman, Daniel, *100 Years of Leeds United: 1919-2019* (Icon Books Ltd, 2019)

Gray, Eddie, *Marching on Together: My Life at Leeds United* (Hodder & Stoughton, 2001)

O'Leary, David, *Leeds United on Trial: The Inside Story of an Astonishing Year* (Little, Brown, 2002)

Rich, Tim, *The Quality of Madness: A Life of Marcelo Bielsa* (Quercus, 2020)

Ridsdale, Peter, *United We Fall: Boardroom Truths About the Beautiful Game* (Pan, 2008)

Saffer, David, *Match of My Life: Leeds* (Know the Score Books, 2006)